BONE REMAINS

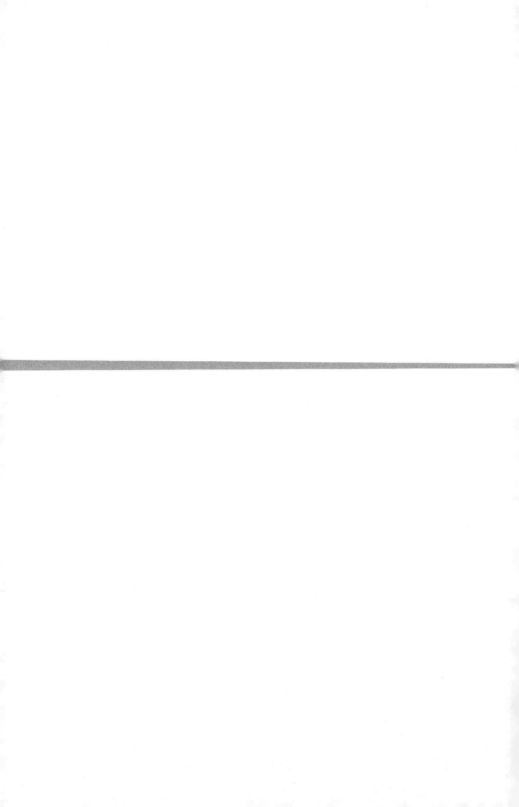

Mary H. Manhein

BONE REMAINS

Cold Cases in Forensic Anthropology

Louisiana State University Press)|(Baton Rouge

Published with the assistance of the Borne Fund

Published by Louisiana State University Press
Copyright © 2013 by Mary H. Manhein
Manufactured in the United States of America
FIRST PRINTING

DESIGNER: *Mandy McDonald Scallan*
TYPEFACE: *Calluna*
PRINTER AND BINDER: *Maple Press*

Library of Congress Cataloging-in-Publication Data
Manhein, Mary H. (Mary Huffman)
  Bone remains : cold cases in forensic anthropology / Mary H. Manhein.
    pages cm
  ISBN 978-0-8071-5323-9 (cloth : alk. paper) — ISBN 978-0-8071-5324-6 (pdf) — ISBN 978-0-8071-5325-3
(epub) — ISBN 978-0-8071-5326-0 (mobi) 1. Forensic anthropology—Case studies. I. Title.
  GN69.8.M35 2014
  599.9—dc23
                                                                                2013010275

The paper in this book meets the guidelines for permanence and durability of the Committee on Production Guidelines for Book Longevity of the Council on Library Resources.∞

For my four grandchildren,
Will, Ben, Mia, and Colin Manhein,
and my two great nieces, Isabelle and Maggie Weaver.

Life is good with you in this world.

Contents

Illustrations

BONE REMAINS

Introduction

Bone Remains is the final installment in a nonfiction trilogy about my career in forensic anthropology. It follows *The Bone Lady* and *Trail of Bones*. I chose the title *Bone Remains* because often bones are all that remain to tell the story of a person's life and death, and because lifeless human bodies are referred to as "remains." This book contains accounts of forensic cases where identifications have been solved and others where, currently, identifications are unsolved. They are among the hundreds and hundreds of cases that have come through the Louisiana State University's Forensic Anthropology and Computer Enhancement Services (FACES) Laboratory, of which I am the creator and director. For more than thirty years, it has been my privilege to help solve the identity of many of these persons and to try to determine what happened to them at or around the time of their death. By highlighting within these pages a few of the unsolved cases from my laboratory experience, I hope to keep them in public view, perhaps to be recognized by someone who can help. Also included in the book is a sample of the many historic cases on which I have worked, giving the reader a glimpse into the past as seen from the perspective of the bone lady.

So often, one of the first questions I am asked is, "How in the world did you get into this business?" It all began one day in the fall of 1980 when I took an anthropology course because it sounded like it would be interesting. I was scheduled to graduate in May 1981 with a degree in English—specifically, creative writing—and I wanted to take a few courses before graduation on topics I had never studied before. The class was called "Old World Archaeology." Less than two weeks into the course, I was hooked on anthropology. I had never had a course that covered the beginnings of human life on earth. The fossils were fascinating to me, and the researchers who spent their lives looking for evidence of the past captivated

1

me with their quests for human origins. By the end of the course, I wanted to change my entire major, one semester away from graduation. I decided instead to go back to school after graduation and get another degree, one in anthropology. I soon found out, though, that you could simply go on to graduate school in a particular field if your grades were good enough and if you made a decent score on the Graduate Record Exams. I was encouraged by Dr. Sharon Goad, the archaeology professor, to take a field school for a couple of weeks in the summer of 1981 to see if I really wanted to go to graduate school in anthropology. I spent two of the longest weeks of my life at Poverty Point in Epps, Louisiana, working in the hot sun all day on a site that was several thousand years old. Digging in that hard clay soil did not inspire me; it only tired me. I was not sure I wanted to pursue archaeology after that, but I knew there were four subdisciplines in anthropology from which to choose: archaeology, biological anthropology, cultural anthropology, and linguistic anthropology. I thought that I would find the right one to fit my interests. I did.

The first semester in graduate school, I took two courses. My children were still young, and I had to take classes that did not conflict with their school schedule. One of those courses was physical anthropology with Dr. Douglas Owsley. That course changed my life forever. Straight out of Tennessee, Dr. Owsley was a new professor at LSU at the time and had begun to contact law enforcement agencies throughout the state to let them know how he could help them with cases of skeletal remains. Most of them had no idea what he was talking about. I volunteered to help in his lab and never left. From 1981 until 1987, I worked with Dr. Owsley as a graduate student and then as a research associate. When he left LSU in 1987 to work at the Smithsonian Institution (along with Murray Marks, a research associate who left soon thereafter), I continued the work of the lab with the help of a graduate student here and there.

By the early 1990s, Eileen Barrow, an artist and sculptor, had begun to work with me part time to create three-dimensional images of the unidentified sets of remains that came through our laboratory. We survived on small grants and the generosity of the agencies with whom we worked. Along the way, we were able to hire Ginesse Listi, a student who had taken an undergraduate course with me in the early 1990s and wanted to have a career in anthropology. Ginny eventually received her master's degree with us and then left to pursue her PhD at Tulane University under Dr. John Vernano. She returned after completing her course work and now is assistant lab director.

Over time, we have added to the FACES Lab team. Helen Bouzon helps with the Missing and Unidentified Database Program and has a master's degree in anthropology, which she earned working with me at LSU. She is a great organizer, and her keen sense of detail has helped us solve many a case over the years. Maria Allaire is a former police officer who was working for a coroner in Durango, Colorado, when she decided to go to graduate school in anthropology. I accepted her as a student, and she received her master's degree at LSU, completing an entomology thesis on decomposition in the mountains of Colorado. No one had conducted research like hers in that part of the country. In fact, Maria even discovered a new hybrid fly, a rare find in entomology. Maria works with the database for missing and unidentified persons, as does Nicole Harris, who became interested in our work after she excavated historic burials with us in a cemetery in north Louisiana. Nicole received her master's in anthropology from the University of Southern Mississippi and not only works with the database group but as an artist also does facial reconstruction work on both forensic and historic cases. Our newest member is Charlana McQuinn, who is from Kentucky and conducted research for her master's thesis there under my supervision. She studied decomposition rates of embalmed and unembalmed remains found on the surface and in burial contexts. Charlana is also an artist and is gaining experience in both forensic case analysis and forensic art. Over the years, scientific illustrator Mary Lee Eggart has provided enormous help with her drawings for our site maps and trauma illustrations, and more than fifty graduate students have assisted us in the lab.

Figure 1. *Clockwise from top,* Research associates Ginesse Listi, Charlana McQuinn, and Helen Bouzon mapping skeletal remains in the woods.

People often ask about our team, how we work together, what's it like to work so closely with that many women, and how, on a daily basis we cope with the considerable amount of tragedy attached to our jobs. One of the things that keeps us going is a sense of humor. A good laugh at ourselves now and then helps carry us through some of the stressful parts of our profession. The diversity of the things that we do makes every single day at work different from every other day. When we come to work in the morning, we have no idea how that day might proceed. It might include law enforcement's discovery of a new case in a field or in the woods somewhere. It might be the day we identify a cold case after one or more agencies from within our state calls us or an agency from out of state contacts us asking that we compare our records with those they have on a missing person. That same day, two or more of us might be teaching a class to undergraduates or graduate students. Or we might be headed toward a workshop out of town where we familiarize law enforcement agencies in Louisiana with our services. We might also be working with our graduate students on one of our many research projects. On rare "quiet days," we have roundtable discussions during lunch that include updates on new and cold cases, subpoenas we have received, and cases that have been in the news and that we might receive.

Since I begin each of my days very early every morning with a cup of coffee and the newspaper, I am the clipper of articles that might impact us. They often come in the form of a small article about a person who jumped off a bridge somewhere in Louisiana, or someone who was reported missing the day before from a boating accident, or some other incident. Perhaps a burned car was found along a road somewhere, and a body was discovered inside. Or someone might have been hunting in the woods and discovered a skull (not nearly as unusual as some might think). Such news is discussed at lunch and, more often than not, becomes part of a new case file on remains we will receive from a law enforcement agency in the next few days. The news article might also assist in establishing a missing-person case on which we will follow up with the appropriate agency.

Some days we spend time listening to a mother share her story of a missing child and how that child is out there somewhere. It doesn't matter if the child is quite young or is an adult, and it doesn't matter if it has been ten days, ten years, or even longer since the child was last seen. That loss, that unbearable loss, is still there. We listen to the family members with the hope that we might be able to help them locate their loved one.

We are ready to travel on a moment's notice to any area in the state, whether for field recovery of victims or to search for a missing person when a tip is provided about where that person's body might be located. Though positive identification of the remains will cause family members pain, that resolution will also help them go on with their lives.

To counter the somber nature of our jobs, we enjoy life to its fullest. We might dress up in our yellow jumpsuits and other protec-

Figure 2. Research associate Nicole Harris searching for human skeletal remains at the base of dug-out well some fifteen feet below the surface.

tive lab clothing and walk in a Mardi Gras parade (thank goodness no one could tell who we were). We might give a lecture about our work to young children or a group of retirees, who all are fascinated with the things we do. We might clown around with our graduate students and play an innocent trick or two on them. At the end of the day, all of us have our own private lives, but in the quest to find persons, identify them, and send them home, we are united.

Much of the lab's growing success is owed to the passage of state legislation in 2006. Then-Governor Kathleen Blanco signed into law a bill that established the Louisiana Repository for Unidentified and Missing Persons Information Program, which would be domiciled at the LSU FACES Laboratory under my direction.

Figure 3. FACES Lab personnel enjoying a moment of humor dressed in hazmat suits.

For several years prior to 2006, my assistants and I had been working toward the goal of gathering into one centralized database information on all unidentified persons found in Louisiana and on all missing persons from Louisiana. Our biggest drawbacks were the lack of funding to support the program and the lack of formal acceptance of our goal. Katrina, the devastating hurricane which paralyzed Louisiana in August 2005, helped to make many people, including members of the Louisiana State Legislature, aware of the importance of such a database.

State funding for our work put us on a whole new level and allowed me to hire research associates. Our job is simple: visit each and every police department, sheriff's office, and coroner's office in the state of Louisiana; gather all data available on cases of unidentified remains in that specific parish and on all missing persons from that parish; and, finally, add the information to a comprehensive database for our state. As of 2013, 150 cases of unidentified persons found in Louisiana are in the database; 20 others in the database are cases found in other states that were sent to Louisiana for analysis. Regarding missing persons from Louisiana, thus far our database contains 200 cases. Another 300 missing-person cases from out of state have been added to our database as out-of-state agencies contacted us to compare records for one of their missing persons. The website associated with the LSU FACES database can be reached by visiting identifyla.lsu.edu.

Additionally, we have submitted all of these cases for unidentified and missing persons to a national database sponsored by the National Institute of Justice (NamUS). The public may find that database at identifyus.org. It includes cases from across the country, and family members can search it to determine if a missing loved one is listed. If not, they can contact the database administrators and have their family member's profile added to the database. They may also review the cases of unidentified persons from across the country to determine if any of them fits the biological profile and time line for their missing loved one.

These databases have become powerful tools for locating individuals. Not only have we submitted biological profiles of our cases to national databases, we have also collected DNA from all unidentified persons found in Louisiana. Moreover, we have begun to collect DNA from consenting family members of missing persons to try to match it with that of a current or future unidentified set of remains. The DNA samples we have collected from both groups have been analyzed by one of the four laboratories with which we have worked over the years—the north Louisiana Criminalistics Laboratory, the St. Tammany Parish Coroner's Office, the Louisiana State Police Crime Laboratory, and Northeast Texas University. In 2011, the Louisiana State Police Crime Laboratory took over the responsibility of handling all of our current and future nuclear DNA cases.

Usually, we need thirteen loci to be defined to have a complete nuclear profile that can be used to identify someone. When nuclear DNA is not sufficient for a complete profile, mitochondrial DNA analysis becomes the go-to technique used to assess the DNA profile of a set of skeletal remains. Mitochondrial DNA, found out in the cytoplasm of the cells, is much more prolific than nuclear DNA and is handed down through generations to sons and daughters from mothers. However, though the son inherits his mother's mitochondrial DNA, he does not pass it down to his own children. If a mother has only sons, her mitochondrial DNA is mostly lost for subsequent generations.

Our DNA profiles for unidentified individuals, as well as family members of missing persons, have been uploaded through the Louisiana State Police Crime Laboratory and through Northeast Texas University (for mitochondrial DNA cases) into CODIS, the National Combined DNA Index System. That FBI system allows searches for what are called "cold-case hits." A cold-case hit occurs when information we have entered into the CODIS system matches the DNA profile of someone who is already in the system. If the person had DNA entered into CODIS through a felony arrest, it's possible a direct hit could be made, though this is a rare occurrence. When family members submit a sample of their DNA to CODIS, their DNA profile is searched only against the unidentified persons in CODIS and not against unknown criminal profiles already present in the system.

The FACES Laboratory has been helped by hundreds of law enforcement agents from across the state and across the country. Those agents offer clear evidence that "yes ma'am" and "no ma'am" have not disappeared from the vocabulary of individuals who give 100 percent effort to solving cases that come through their agencies. Too numerous to mention by name, they remain passionate about their responsibility to their communities. Many of them have gone out of their way to help us in field-recovery situations with travel support on four-wheelers, in boats, in mini-trucks, and in RVs, while providing us with food, drinks, and portable facilities. They have lightened our load with a joke or two here or there and have eased the harsh conditions under which we sometimes work, such as sloshing through the woods, in the winter, in the rain!

Finally, though many people contribute to the ongoing success of the LSU FACES Lab, the support from our families, our university, and our state makes our work possible. For that we are grateful.

1. In the Deep Woods

The hunters were walking in the deep woods of north Louisiana. The man and his son stumbled across what appeared to be human bones, though they seemed too small to represent an adult. The bones were just a few feet off a narrow, unpaved road used only by the members of a private hunting club. The man quickly called the sheriff's office to report the gruesome discovery.

October 8, 2010, 10:30 p.m. The phone was ringing. Something was wrong somewhere. Was it my family or was it my job? Nervously, on the third ring, I picked it up. A coroner needed a forensic anthropology team.

Mr. Raymond Rouse, coroner of Catahoula Parish in north central Louisiana, had asked his wife and full-time assistant, Mrs. Rouse, to call me. They needed help, Mrs. Rouse said, and they needed it right away. She had been given my name and telephone number by the Louisiana State Police. She relayed how the hunter and his son had been walking in an isolated, wooded area of their sparsely populated parish earlier in the day and had discovered a set of what they thought were human skeletal remains. Mrs. Rouse also went on to say that the sheriff of the parish, James Kelly, had consulted with the coroner, and they both agreed that they needed help with the case, the likes of which they had never seen before and hoped to never see again. Mrs. Rouse explained that they thought the bones might belong to a fairly young individual and that the sex might be a female because the teeth had braces on them and the bands on the braces were pink.

Though quite a few of the remains had already been recovered when they called me, I asked them to please stop the recovery work and put a guard on the site for the rest of the night and until we could get there the next day. I told Mrs. Rouse that our team from the LSU Forensic Anthropology and Computer Enhancement Services, or FACES, Laboratory, would be there the following morning around 10:00 a.m.

Since we had not worked with Catahoula's coroner before, I explained to Mrs. Rouse that we were trained in recovery and analysis of human skeletal remains and that training and experience could be extremely important in months to come, especially if the case turned out to be a homicide. Mr. Rouse, the coroner, agreed to hold the site.

I hung up the phone and immediately called Ginny Listi and told her to put together a recovery team, and, especially, to round up a couple of our graduate students to assist with the case. Experience in the field and in the lab is the only way students who study to be forensic anthropologists can ever call themselves that. They absolutely must have such experience because no book learning in the world will ever make a biological anthropologist with a master's degree or a PhD into a forensic anthropologist without on-the-job training. Every case is different; we just did not know at the time how different this one would be. I went to bed that night but did not sleep well, knowing that we had a three-hour drive ahead of us the next day and the possibility of a child victim.

Thank goodness children's cases are rare in our line of work, but even at that, I can see the handful or so of them on which I have worked in the last thirty years as though they happened yesterday.

Around 10 a.m. on October 9, 2010, FACES Lab personnel including Ginny and two graduate students, Charlana McQuinn and Valerie Kauffeld, and I pulled into Harrisonburg, Louisiana. A town of approximately 2,000 people, Harrisonburg is the largest town in Catahoula Parish and is the parish seat. The parish has a population of approximately 10,000. The town and the parish have a very low crime rate, with the greatest crime in the area usually associated with someone doing "a little drugs."

First, as pre-determined, we went to the small stationery shop from which the coroner operated. In Louisiana, we have a coroner's system, not a medical examiner's system. All coroners are elected by the citizens in their respective parishes. Most parishes, especially those with large, metropolitan areas, have coroners who are medical doctors, a few of whom perform their own autopsies. The first requirement that qualifies a person to run for coroner in any parish is related to time lived in that parish. Also, a citizen can run for coroner in a parish only if a medical doctor in that parish does not wish to run. If a medical doctor runs, that automatically cancels out any non-medical candidate. Five parishes in Louisiana have non-medical doctors as their coroners. Catahoula is one of the five.

At Mr. Rouse's office, he explained to me that the human skeletal remains that had already been recovered were being held at the sheriff's office and that he would take us there. Upon arrival at the sheriff's office, we were introduced to Sheriff James Kelly and his staff. I examined the remains in the paper bags and noted that investigators were correct in assuming that they belonged to a young individual, probably between the ages of ten and fourteen. Though I did not make a final determination about the sex of the young person since sex determination can be difficult in a juvenile, the pink bands on the dental braces suggested female.

We left the sheriff's office and headed back into an isolated area that was heavily wooded. Officers explained that the dirt road meandered throughout the hills in that region and that one could get completely lost if unfamiliar with the area. My antenna went up immediately, and I thought, "Whoever dropped off this child knew this area."

The remains were unusually close to the old hunting road. The general area from which most of the bones had been recovered exhibited dark staining in the soil, and the decomposition residue confirmed that the staining indicated the spot where the body had decomposed. Though the sheriff's deputies had already picked up most of the remains, I divided our team into two groups, and we began our recovery. I stayed at the site where the body had first rested. Charlana, Ginny, and Valerie headed to the surrounding woods with bright colored flags to mark any new evidence. The decomposing body had attracted carnivores, and parts of the body had been moved by the animals. Immediately, the search team began to call out that they had found human hair, a lot of human hair, and several bones. Since we had completed a mental inventory of the major bones that were missing prior to entering the woods, we knew approximately what bones were still unaccounted for.

Throughout the rest of the morning and into the late afternoon, we mapped scattered remains, photographed and collected those remains, and searched for more. As a general rule at recovery scenes, if we have found no additional bones or artifacts related to the case for a couple of hours, we halt the recovery effort. In this case, we completed our work around 3:30 p.m., having found nothing new for some time.

Sheriff Kelly asked if I thought it would be a good idea to call in extra help to search for the remains. "Extra help" in his mind meant the Federal Bureau of Investigation. I told him he should feel comfortable asking for additional help from anyone he felt could add assistance, a statement that later complicated jurisdiction in the case and led to a disagreement between the FBI and me. Before we left Harrisonburg, Sheriff Kelly told us they had no one at all who was missing, much less a child.

The coroner released the remains to me that day, and we drove back to our lab in Baton Rouge. We told him that we would begin our analysis on Monday morning, October 11. On Monday, we x-rayed all the remains, looking for any foreign objects associated with the bone and obtaining good x-rays of the teeth with our portable machine called the Nomad.

We then assessed the skeleton for ancestry. Ancestry in adults can be challenging to say the least. It can be even more challenging in children's remains. In adults, we often rely on information provided to us by metric analysis of the skull, whereby we take as many as thirty-four measurements across the skull and plug those measurements into a software package known as Fordisc. However, Fordisc is not designed to determine ancestry in a child. Yet, by the age of twelve, or sometimes even younger, some facial features and other information can provide an idea of the ancestry. In this case, the texture and appearance of the hair and general shape of the facial bones suggested that we had a white child.

Assessing the sex of a set of skeletal remains when the child is young is a difficult thing to do. Distinctions between the sexes usually are not evident until puberty (and this child appeared to just be entering puberty). However, we felt that the pink bands on the braces the child was wearing and the unusually long hair suggested the victim was a female. Of course, if it became necessary, DNA analysis would be able to confirm if the child was a male or a female.

Our third piece of the profile puzzle was age. For those cases below the age of eighteen years, the growth and development of the teeth are the best way to age a child. Our dental x-rays suggested that we had a child somewhere between the ages of ten and fourteen. We x-rayed the teeth and assessed the stage of development of the permanent molars. Humans have two sets of teeth, the deciduous teeth, of which there are twenty, and the permanent teeth, numbering thirty-two. The three permanent molars in each quadrant of the mouth develop and erupt at different times in the life of a child. The first permanent molar erupts around six years of age, the second around twelve years, and the third around eighteen. This child had twelve-year molars which had erupted, giving us a clue that, minimally, she most likely was somewhere between ten and fourteen.

We had our general profile, white female probably between ten and fourteen years of age, the same one we had provided the sheriff in his office. However, we would not make the final call on age. That decision would be made by Dr. Robert Barsley, the LSU odontologist with whom I have worked for more than twenty-five years. I knew that Bob could provide a more concise estimate and that more than likely he could tell us a heck of a lot about the dental braces. We scheduled the meeting for a few days later and turned to trauma.

We examined all of the bones for the three different kinds of trauma we assess: antemortem (before death); postmortem (after death); and perimortem (at or around the time of death). We found both perimortem trauma and postmortem trauma on the bones.

On Friday, October 22, 2010, Ginny and I traveled to the LSU Dental School in New Orleans to discuss the child's case with Dr. Barsley. Dr. Barsley introduced us to Dr. Paul Armbruster, pediatric dentist, and the two of them began to explain the orthodontic treatment present on the child's teeth. Dr. Armbruster noted that the braces suggested that the orthodontist apparently was performing traditional mechanics to create space for an upper right, impacted canine to drop into proper alignment. Specifically, an effort was being made to unwind the rotation of tooth #4 (upper right, second premolar) in a counter-clockwise direction through the use of wire and brackets. This was in conjunction with using a "power chain" (rubber band) on numbers 7–10 (upper incisors) to bring them closer together. The power chains were pink. Both Armbruster and Barsley said this suggested a female. They also noted that spacing of the teeth suggested the treatment was in its early stages. Additionally, power chains typically are replaced every month or so. In this case, the power chains appeared to be quite new, suggesting that the child had recently seen an orthodontist, an important clue.

Next, the dentists moved to identify the exact maker of the braces themselves. They determined that the braces were American Orthodontics brand and that the wire on them was nickel titanium. This particular wire is flexible and thermally sensitive. Different manufacturers of dental braces are known by the color codes they use on the different quadrants of the metal brackets on the teeth. For example, tooth #4 had a black quadrant identification mark on its distal gingival tie wing, and #12 had a green quadrant identification mark on its distal gingival tie wing. The colors were consistent with those used by American Orthodontics.

Finally, the child appeared to have sealants on various teeth. Sealants often are used when a tooth has the beginnings of a small cavity and the dentist wishes to prevent any further deterioration of the tooth.

Dental x-rays showed that the child's twelve-year molars were complete and that the eighteen-year molars (wisdom teeth) were only in the crown complete stage, meaning that the formation of the root of the wisdom teeth had not yet occurred.

Best assessment from Drs. Barsley and Armbruster: more than likely, the victim was between twelve and thirteen years of age.

Not over thirteen. Female. White. Armed with three of the most important profile markers by late Friday afternoon of October 22, I mulled over the case all that weekend. Adding considerable urgency to the identification was a phone call from the FBI in which the agent insisted that the remains be sent to the National Center for Missing and Exploited Children for a facial reconstruction to aid with the identity. I balked. I knew that the center (NCMEC) was very capable of completing a facial reconstruction on the unidentified child, but I also knew that our laboratory was just as capable and had many years of experience in doing just that. I stood my ground, and though I feel certain I made multiple people unhappy with me, the coroner for Catahoula Parish decided that the remains should stay with our laboratory in Louisiana. The coroner of each parish in Louisiana controls curation of remains in any such case.

I was determined to identify the child. In fact, perhaps a facial reconstruction would not be necessary. Combined with the information from the Catahoula Sheriff's Office that "no one from their area had been reported missing," I decided to try a new tack on Monday. At noon on Monday, October 25, just one work day after consulting with Drs. Barsley and Armbruster, two of my research associates and I sat down after lunch, and I said to them, "We will identify this child today." I asked Nicole Harris and Helen Bouzon to go online and find any female child missing nationally who fit into a general age category of eleven to fifteen. They both began to search. Nicole handed me a small stack of four printouts. The one that stood out was the flyer for a child named Lexis Kaye Roberts, twelve years of age, who had last been seen Labor Day weekend, 2010, when she left town with her mother, Suellen Roberts, and her mother's friend, Thomas Steven Sanders, for a brief holiday. None of them had been seen since.

The photo of Lexis that was posted on the missing-children site did not show a smile, so I could not tell if her upper right canine was present. I then asked Helen to go online and find something, anything, on this child that showed a smiling photo. Everything fit; I just knew that she was the victim. No more than five minutes later, Helen came across a video of Lexis that was made in Arizona and showed her smiling face. Her upper right canine was missing. I knew then that all we had to do was confirm it. Our victim was Lexis Kaye Roberts.

The missing-persons flyer on the web noted that Lexis and her mother, Suellen Roberts, had left their home on Labor Day weekend in the company of Thomas Steven Sanders. I asked Nicole to find something that would link Sanders to east central Louisiana. There had to be a connection because I kept thinking of how remote the area was and that whoever had placed Lexis there had to have had a connection to the area. Nicole found a notation on line that said that Sanders had formerly lived in Louisiana.

Next, I asked Helen to get me the telephone number of the detective in the county in Arizona from which Lexis and her mom had been reported missing—Coconino County. Ultimately, I spoke with Lt. Tim Cornelius, and he was invaluable in helping to positively identify Lexis. I explained the situation to him and told him I needed dental x-rays for Lexis. He put me in contact with her dentist, Dr. Daniel Sims. Dr. Sims and I went over the records over the phone, and he noted that the space for her canine and other dental fillings exactly matched what we had. However, he said that he had not put braces on Lexis. We had to have that information. I called Lt. Cornelius back, and he contacted Lexis's grandmother, who provided him with the name of the orthodontist who had placed braces on Lexis. A phone call to orthodontist Dr. Dave Smith in Las Vegas resulted in orthodontic records being sent to Dr. Barsley and me. Dr. Smith confirmed that Lexis had gotten her braces on June 7, 2010, and her last appointment with him was September 2, 2010, just three days before she left town. Dental records and x-rays which he forwarded to Dr. Barsley and me confirmed by 9:30 p.m. central time that day that the child's skeletal remains found in Catahoula Parish in east central Louisiana were those of Lexis Kaye Roberts. She was over fifteen hundred miles from home.

Authorities began a search for Sanders and Lexis's mother, Suellen, and Suellen's 2001 Kia four-door sedan. In doing so, they came across some surprising information. First, Sanders had once lived in and around Harrisonburg, the Louisiana connection. Secondly, and even more surprising, Thomas Steven Sanders had been declared dead in Mississippi in 1994 after disappearing in 1987. On Sunday, November 13, 2010, Sanders was arrested at a truck stop in Gulfport, Mississippi. He was in possession of Suellen Roberts's Kia sedan. On November 15, 2010, authorities recovered a body off Interstate 40 near Seligman, Arizona. The body was identified as Suellen Roberts on or around December 22, 2010. Sanders is in prison facing kidnapping and murder charges. He has pleaded not guilty. What happened to Lexis was revealed in her bones but cannot be discussed publicly before Sanders's trial.

This is one of those cases that will haunt me for a very long time. Lexis Kaye Roberts was just a baby who will never grow up, never have a first date, never go to college, never get married and have babies of her own. Of course, the family was absolutely devastated by what happened to Lexis and her mother, Suellen. Lexis's great-aunt, who lives in New Hampshire, wrote to me about Lexis, and I wanted to share her note with others who have lost a loved one: "She visited me summers and enjoyed her respite from the desert of Nevada, hiking the White Mountains and swimming the Atlantic Ocean in New Hampshire. Life will not be the same without her. She was very inquisitive, loved iCarly, the color purple, was looking forward to learning to play the Viola (her choice), and some day wanted to own a Toyota Prius. And she loved angels, which she now has become."

2. Long Journey Home

I t was the summer of 1975. Popular music was spinning great stories of broken hearts and bad love. Carly Simon's earlier hit, "You're so Vain" was still riding a wave of success on the radio, and the Eagles were grinding out "One of These Nights," which would become an overnight success of its own. Antonio Barajas, a young Hispanic male from Texas, and a friend were traveling through western Louisiana for reasons unknown. After a brief sighting in Many, Louisiana, in DeSoto Parish, Barajas and his friend vanished. A short time later, his friend's body showed up in a city dump. More than likely, he had been murdered. Still no sign of Barajas.

Four years later, in 1979, a set of human skeletal remains was found in a rural dump in Bossier Parish, miles away from Many, Louisiana. Those skeletal remains were taken to the coroner in Caddo Parish, Dr. George McCormick, for analysis. At that time, McCormick's assistant was Dr. William Rodriguez, a forensic anthropologist out of Tennessee who would later go on to work at the AFIP (Armed Forces Institute of Pathology). Rodriguez assessed the remains, noting that they appeared to represent the bones of a young male whose ancestry, or race, was somewhat ambiguous. No positive identification was made.

During the early 1980s, a few cases had trickled down to LSU in Baton Rouge from the Caddo Parish coroner in order for Rodriguez to consult with another forensic anthropologist at LSU. This case became one of those. Rodriguez asked for assistance in trying to sort out the ancestry of the young man. Ancestry often can be one of the most elusive components of a biological profile. In this particular case, it proved quite daunting.

When the case came to LSU in 1982, I was in my second year of graduate school, and Dr. Douglas Owsley was the university's forensic anthropologist. Owsley, like Rodriguez, was a freshly minted PhD out of the University of Tennessee in Knoxville who had studied under Dr. William Bass, creator of the Anthropological Research Facility there, better known today in the popular press as the "Body Farm." Owsley evaluated the remains, immediately noting that the human bones found in Bossier Parish had a shiny patina to them. No odor was associated with the bones, suggesting that the young man had been dead for several years when first discovered. Cranial measurements and non metric characteristics indicated that he was a white individual who also possessed Native American features. The sutures, or joints, in his skull were complex, which meant that, rather than forming somewhat straight lines across the top, sides, and back of the skull at various locations, as most of those of white or black ancestry might do, his sutures meandered across the surface of the skull, forming intricate patterns. Additionally, he had small, extra bones associated with some of the skull's sutures. These bones, or ossicles, are referred to as wormian bones. Both the complex suture pattern and the wormian bones suggested the young man might be of Native American ancestry.

Owsley thought the young man was somewhere between twenty-two and twenty-eight years of age. He came to this conclusion by evaluating age-related changes that occur on several strategic areas on the skeleton, including features on the pubic bones and auricular surfaces of the os coxae, or pelvis. Once a person reaches adulthood, those surfaces change, or degenerate, throughout an individual's lifetime, and standards have been created to suggest certain age ranges for different stages of degeneration. Still, no leads resulted from this analysis, and the unidentified man's skeletal remains were curated in the section of the lab marked "unidentified."

For more than a quarter of a century, the bones of the young adult male rested in a curation box in the forensic anthropology laboratory at LSU. All hope for getting him identified had long since faded. He was just one among a number of cases that had been sent to LSU by various state agencies over the years, beginning in the early 1980s.

In the 1980s, forensic anthropology was still in its infancy. Fewer than fifty persons across the entire United States carried that title; fewer still helped to identify people on a regular basis.

By 2005, twenty-six years had passed since the bones had been found. Owsley had been gone from LSU for eighteen years, but I was still here. As early as 2004, I had been trying to develop a comprehensive database for our unidentified cases. With a small grant, I was able to take a bone sample from the young, unidentified male and have it analyzed at a DNA laboratory. A DNA sample from an unidentified person can include a tooth and a small section from a long bone, or perhaps small sections from two different long bones. Also, we have recently found that any site across the skeleton where muscles attach is a good site for potential DNA retrieval, especially in the general area of the frontal and parietal bones of the skull. Those samples are taken in a near-sterile environment and are hand-carried to a DNA laboratory. Subsequently, the DNA profile of the unidentified person is uploaded to the national CODIS database.

Though the young man found in Bossier Parish in 1979 was a case that was more than a quarter of a century old, a solid nuclear DNA profile was still present in the bone and was of a quality that could provide useable information. A useable DNA profile typically requires twelve to thirteen loci (with the loci representing specific areas or "sites" on a chromosome where genetic markers used for identification are located) to be entered into CODIS. In some situations, there are exceptions to the minimum number of loci required. Also, if a certain number of loci match (and this number can vary), additional testing can be undertaken to determine whether the presumed positive identification is valid. In the case of the young man who was found in 1979, when his DNA profile was entered into CODIS, no cold-case hit was made.

In 2007, I asked Eileen Barrow, imaging specialist, to create a three-dimensional, clay facial reconstruction for the young man. I was heading to north Louisiana to conduct a workshop for law enforcement personnel in that region of the state, and I thought it would be great to show them our case from 1982 just to see if it would strike a chord with someone. I took the facial reconstruction to Shreveport for the workshop, but no one even remembered the case. How could they? Many of the young officers in the workshop probably were not even born when the skeletal remains were found.

I brought the clay facial reconstruction back to our laboratory at LSU and set it on a counter in the lab. A few months later, Detective Robert Davidson of DeSoto Parish just happened to be in my lab to consult on an entirely different case when he saw the facial reconstruction sitting on the table. "What's that, Mary?" he asked. I told him the story of the cold case and how I had taken the reconstruction to Shreveport, hoping that area law enforcement personnel might be able to assist us with getting the young man identified, but to no avail.

Then I said, "Why?" Detective Davidson answered with the words we love to hear.

"He looks familiar to me." I almost fell off the stool when he said that. Shivers went up my back. I will never forget it. He said that he had been working on a new website for the sheriff's office and that they had a very old case of a young man who was last seen in their parish back in 1975. He had just put up a picture of Antonio Barajas on their website, a young Hispanic male from Texas, and thought our image looked a little like him. I went over the details of our case with Detective Davidson, telling him how the young man in our lab had been found in a garbage dump in 1979 not too far from his parish. He noted that Barajas and a friend had come to Louisiana in 1975. The friend's body, also found in a garbage dump, but not in the same one, had been recovered not too long after the two young men had disappeared. Barajas had never been found. I was so excited I could hardly stand it. I asked him to please go home and check it out and get back with me. He did.

He called a day or so later and said that he went through the old files and found the names of Mr. Barajas's family but had no idea where they were in 2007. Davidson made phone calls to various agencies, put ads in Texas papers, and waited. A short time later, Barajas's family was found in West Texas. His mother was still alive

Figure 4. Clay facial reconstruction of unidentified male.

Figure 5. Antonio Barajas— identified after thirty-two years.

and was in her nineties. He had brothers and sisters who were still living also.

Detective Davidson made arrangements to obtain the family's DNA, and, within a few weeks, we had a positive identification on our case. Antonio Barajas went home after thirty-two years. His case is the oldest case thus far for which we have solved the identity. Barajas's mom spoke with Detective Davidson on the phone and said, "I can't believe someone was still looking for my son, after all these years." Figure 4 is the facial reconstruction created by Eileen Barrow for our unknown victim. Figure 5 is a DeSoto Parish sheriff's website photo of the young man, Antonio Barajas, who had been missing for 32 years. Though not an exact match, the image and the story captured Detective Davidson's attention—just what we want the images to do, whether they absolutely look like the person or not. What we did not know at the time was that, within a matter of a few months, Detective Davidson would help us to solve another cold case from his parish.

As we make our way across the state of Louisiana, notifying various agencies of our work, we continue to encounter unsolved cases that involve human skeletal remains. This particular one came to us in a roundabout way when we were allowed to collect all the human bones we could find in the Bossier Pathology Center after Dr. George McCormick, the Caddo Parish coroner who ran the lab, died unexpectedly in 2006. A human cranium from the Bossier lab had a lab reference number that led us to DeSoto Parish—and Detective Davidson. When we contacted Davidson about the case, he, too, became excited about the possibility of identifying the person, especially because he was still riding high from the positive results of the thirty-two-year-old case of Antonio Barajas with which we had assisted.

This case was very different from Mr. Barajas's case in that it was just a cranium, the skull without the lower jaw. It had been curated for more than twenty years in the Bossier lab, and a records search by Davidson revealed he was the officer on duty back in 1984 when the cranium was found along a rural road in DeSoto Parish.

At the FACES Lab, we assessed the partial skull for age, sex, and ancestry. Our profile was that of a young, adult, black male. In looking through the sheriff's records, Davidson found a missing-person report on a young man by the name of Ricky Maxie. Davidson contacted Maxie's sister, Joyce Maxie, and explained what we were doing and asked if she would be willing to provide a DNA sample to rule her in or out as a relative of the person represented by the skull. Of course, she agreed.

Two months or so later, we were able to tell her that the cranium that was found almost twenty-two years prior was that of her brother, Ricky. The family had hoped beyond all hope that Ricky would come home some day. Joyce Maxie had never given up. She just did not know that it would take so long to find her brother. None of his other remains has been found.

3. A "Princess" of Thebes

She lay in a glass-enclosed case in the center of the room. Footfalls tapped softly against the highly polished floor as visitors surrounded her exhibit in the small museum adjacent to the Mississippi River in Baton Rouge, Louisiana. For over fifty years she had rested there, but it was not her home, and those visitors were not her people. Reportedly, she was "a princess of Thebes" and had been brought to Louisiana in 1964 when the museum in Philadelphia where she had previously resided shut its doors. She was a relic; that much was certain. Where she had come from and her personal history would take some time to understand. But time was all she had.

At least two thousand years old, she had lived during the glory days of Egypt's past. She was a mummy, one among approximately one hundred that had been shipped to the United States, mostly during the early part of the twentieth century when it was fashionable for society folk to have an "unwrapping" as part of their frequent soirees when they were bored silly.

In the 1970s, I would take my two young sons on an occasional summer day to the museum in Baton Rouge, where we would admire the mummy in her case. My sons and I were quite taken by the idea that the mummy had come from a place where great stone pyramids, exotic statues, and other tributes to ancient pharaohs beckoned to us from across the centuries. Well preserved, the linen wrappings with accompanying cartonnage indicated that she was from the Ptolemaic period. The Ptolemaic dated from 332 BC, when Alexander the Great of Macedon conquered Egypt, to 30 BC, ending with the death of Cleopatra the Seventh.

In 2007, almost thirty years after my sons and I last visited the museum together, I received a request from the current museum curator, Ms. Elizabeth Weinstein, that piqued my curiosity immediately. She wanted to know if the LSU FACES Laboratory would be interested in examining the mummy and providing the Louisiana Art and Science Museum with as much information about the mummy as possible. Renovation of various displays and exhibits at the museum included an effort to display the mummy with accurate detail. Could FACES Lab personnel confirm age and sex and, perhaps, provide an opinion on illness or injury? I knew we could tell Elizabeth many things, even with the restrictions that allowed us only to x-ray and photograph the mummy. In fact, we could not actually touch the mummy unless we wore gloves; even then, touching had to be at a minimum. Of course, we agreed.

It was a hot summer day when we drove to the museum to pick up the mummy. Though I had analyzed thousands of skeletons in the past, very few held the draw of this mysterious lady. Part of the reason was simple: how often does one have the chance to look inside a mummy's linen wrappings, even with simply an x-ray machine?

When we arrived at the museum, Mr. Lance Harris, one of the museum curators, was waiting for us. We gently wrapped the mummy in plastic and placed it on a plywood board to support it for our short trip to the LSU FACES Lab. The five-mile drive was made in less than fifteen minutes. We backed up to the loading dock at the Howe-Russell Geoscience Building and drew only a few students to the sight. Since we often unload modern forensic cases at the same dock, "just another dead body" seemed to be the general consensus among the few students who paused for a moment and then drifted away.

Carefully, we unloaded the mummy from the van and moved her into our x-ray room at the FACES Laboratory. Quite frankly, I was in awe. Here was the mummy my sons and I had looked at in a glass-enclosed case all of those years ago. To have the chance to learn more about her would be the opportunity of a lifetime. Assisting me would be Dr. Jonathan Elias, an Egyptologist from Philadelphia, members of the LASM museum staff, and the research associates of the FACES Lab. The mummy could not remain with

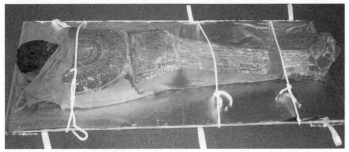

Figure 6. Close-up of 2,000-year-old Theban mummy's cartonnage with Ptolemaic images.

Figure 7. Close-up of mummy's face.

us overnight; therefore, we had to work swiftly and efficiently to x-ray her so that she could be returned to the museum the same day.

The first thing we did was to remove the plastic from around her cartonnage and then photograph her from every angle we could within the confines of the x-ray room. Our initial description was brief. We had before us an adult-size mummy encased in a linen cartonnage with a full shock of curly hair (figures 6 and 7). The teeth were present and fully visible, the mummified tissue of the lips having retracted, revealing the tongue. In fact, the mouth gaped open.

We took many photographs of the mummy, knowing full well this was more than likely the one and only time we would have a real Egyptian mummy in our lab. Our lab had hosted hundreds and hundreds of individuals, some even older than the mummy who now lay on our x-ray machine, but few as intriguing in terms of ancient history.

We set the x-ray machine to our standard setting for fully tissued individuals, 60 Kvs, 100 Mas, 1/2 second. We began with the head. As lead principal investigator for the FACES Laboratory, I usually operate the x-ray machine. I punched the button on the control unit, aware that I was about to see inside a skull that was at least two thousand years old. As we ran the exposed x-ray film through the digital developer, we moved down the body with the next cassette, x-raying as we went along until we reached and x-rayed the feet.

What were we looking for? Over the years, many graves were looted in Egypt, and artifacts were routinely removed. However, mummies from those violated graves showed evidence of harm when researchers recovered them—body parts strewn about, the cartonnage ripped open at the chest, signs of disarray. "Our" mummy's cartonnage was completely intact and had no outward signs of looting damage. So we hoped to see perhaps an amulet or two, maybe a scarab, or even a bracelet of some kind. We also hoped to see evidence of the techniques used in mummification, maybe some signs of disease, or even a gold-encrusted ring or two. Our imaginations went wild.

As we developed the x-rays, we were in for some surprises, but not the kind we had anticipated. First, and perhaps foremost, "she" was a "he." Radiographic details clearly revealed a pelvis only a male could possess. A small pelvic inlet, a narrow, sciatic notch, an acute subpubic angle all indicated male (figure 8). Also, an informal survey of practicing forensic anthropologists who are members of the Society of Forensic Anthropologists (SOFA) and who viewed the x-ray of the pelvic region resulted in almost 100 percent agreement with our conclusion of male. Additionally, in assessing an x-ray of the skull, a squarish chin, large mastoid processes, and flared gonion (region at the back of the lower jaw) added credence to our assessment. Finally, as was typical for males (except for royalty), the hands were

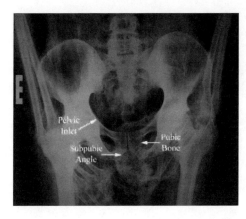

Figure 8. X-ray of mummy's hips; arrows point to features confirming male sex designation.

placed together over the pubic region, called the pendant position. Generally, females' hands were placed at their sides. A subsequent, unplanned CT scan confirmed the sex by revealing male soft-tissue anatomy.

Next, we wanted to look at his age. Though not entirely appropriate for someone as ancient as our mummy, modern standards of growth and development were used to estimate age at death based on what the radiographic images revealed. He appeared to be a young adult, most likely between twenty-five and thirty years of age. His third molars, or wisdom teeth, had completed their development (suggesting a minimum age of eighteen). Apparent fusion of the epiphyses (growth regions) of his medial clavicles had occurred (confirming an age greater than twenty-two). His sacrum was only partially fused to the coccyx (suggesting an age under thirty years). Other epiphyses (regions on the ends of long and short bones, especially) in his skeleton appeared to be fused. Finally, the absence of osteoarthritis in his vertebral column, his knee joints, and other joints confirmed his youth. We had a sex and we had an age.

Our analysis of pathology and evaluation of general health of the mummy were somewhat limited. Only his face, part of his head, and some of his teeth were visible. Dental wear, defined as a combination of attrition and abrasion, was present on the incisive or occlusal

Figure 9. Close-up of mummy's closely cropped, curly hair.

surfaces of his anterior and visible posterior teeth. Egyptians ate bread, a lot of bread. In fact, they were known as "artophagians," or eaters of bread. That bread contained considerable inorganic contaminants that included sand (or quartz), mica, feldspar, and other minerals. Those gritty contaminants clearly affected the biting and chewing surfaces of their teeth. The occlusal, or biting, surface of the young male's teeth was heavily worn, a fact consistent with a diet with a lot of grit in it.

Another consideration of health included the tibiae. Visible in x-rays of his tibiae was one region that might have been the remnant of a remodeled Harris Line. Harris Lines occur during the period of growth and development of the individual when illness or malnutrition interrupts that growth and it does not proceed at a normal pace. This cessation of growth, and subsequent continuation of growth, may occur multiple times in affected bones and is viewed on an x-ray as somewhat dense, white lines near the distal and/or proximal ends of the bones. Seen most often in the femora and tibiae, through time, these lines of provisional calcification may remodel and completely disappear as the person ages. This mummy had one Harris Line, hardly an indicator of poor health.

Considering both his dental health and other aspects of the skeleton, he appeared to be a healthy young man at death.

Though hair often is not preserved, this mummy had a shock of short hair, arranged in curls reminiscent of the Greek influence in Egypt at the time (figure 9). His hair was reddish brown, though the color could be a result of burial preparation. Based on a heel-to-crown measurement, he was approximately five feet seven inches tall.

What about trauma? As forensic anthropologists, we look at three kinds of trauma: antemortem (before death, such as a healed, broken arm); postmortem trauma, trauma after death (such as animal gnawing marks); or perimortem trauma, trauma that occurs at or around the time of death and may be related to the cause of death.

No evidence of antemortem trauma was found on the young man's skeleton. However, possible perimortem trauma was obvious. This mummy had a total of seventeen breaks in his ribs (arrows in figure 10 point to breaks). Some of the breaks are near the vertebral ends of the ribs (in the case of left and right first ribs), while others are found closer to the mid-point of the ribs. This breakage suggests a crushing blow to the chest region (a flailed chest), possibly anterior to posterior or even side to side. Had these been antemortem injuries, one would expect to see a smoothing or rounding of the edges of the breaks in the x-ray and/or slightly dense, white lines near the ends of the bones. One or both of these features would be evidence for remodeling or knitting of the bones had they begun to heal. No such healing was evident.

Could these broken ribs be postmortem in origin? It is always possible. Again, grave looting was extensive in ancient Egypt, and many mummies show evidence of postmortem damage to their thoracic regions especially, to their skulls, and to other areas of the skeleton. However, if the broken ribs on this mummy had been postmortem from plundering, one would expect to see damage to the linen wrappings. As noted earlier, the linen wrappings were in excellent condition.

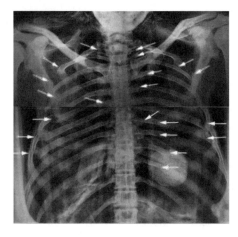

Figure 10. Chest x-ray of mummy with arrows pointing to multiple perimortem fractures.

What happened to the young man after death can be understood only partially. This mummy was not prepared for burial in the typical Egyptian fashion. In the traditional mummification process, the person's brain was removed by inserting an iron hook into the nostril and ethmoid, moving it around somewhat to separate the cerebral material, and then scooping it out with a spatula. In looking at his thoracic region, at least some of his organs were still intact. Even as late as the Ptolemaic period, removal of certain organs was still part of the mummification process. Additionally, neither the arms nor the legs had been wrapped separately prior to doing the generalized "body" wrap.

Mummification techniques did become somewhat sloppy in the later periods; yet, other evidence offers intriguing possibilities regarding the young man's body at the time of mummification.

Though somewhat difficult to see in a photograph, arrows point to something most unusual. Incorporated into the mummy's wrappings is evidence for what may be a type of ancient stretcher (figure 11). According to Dr. Elias, the Egyptologist, the stretcher is composed of four struts running longitudinally from the upper back downward to the ankles. The struts have a faceted appearance in cross-section which is comparable to material found in other mum-

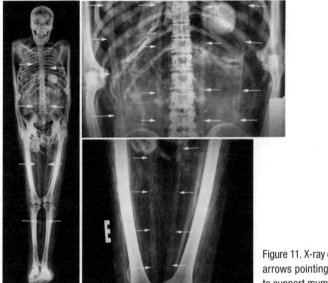

Figure 11. X-ray of mummy with arrows pointing to reeds used to support mummy's stretcher.

mies identified as palm struts. In this case, the struts are spaced eight to nine centimeters apart and converge at the ankle level. Two transverse palm struts are secured at the level of the upper back and at the level of the upper pelvis. The stretcher has been incorporated into the linen body wrap. The bandages are interwoven among the longitudinal struts to form an integrated whole. The general impression is that the body was carried on the stretcher.

Our conclusion was that this young man may have been injured at some distance from home; he may have even died at that location. Following his death, a makeshift stretcher was created to get him back home for a proper burial. Once there, the processing technicians realized that natural mummification had already desiccated the tissues, and that traditional mummification techniques would prove useless. They made a decision. They placed his hands over his pubic region and they incorporated his entire body and the stretcher into his linen wrappings.

Of note, no grave goods, such as amulets, bracelets, or rings were

Figure 12. 2-D facial reconstruction of mummy's appearance in life.

present on the mummy, suggesting someone of lower social status than a prince.

One final request was made by the museum curators. They asked if we would give the mummy a face. Eileen Barrow, imaging specialist at the FACES laboratory, used an anterior/posterior x-ray of his skull to assist in creating a two-dimensional approximation of what he may have looked like in life. She had to reposition the mandible to more closely represent its proper anatomical position. Next, she added tissue depth markers to strategic locations across the face and then created a line drawing of his face—our Prince of Thebes (figure 12).

In recent years, each new discovery of mummies in Egypt claims international attention and evokes images of gods and goddesses, pharaohs and queens, everyday citizens, and movie magic. Yet, right under our noses, in warehouses and local museums may be evidence for untold, fascinating stories of that ancient civilization's culture.

This "Prince" of Thebes now resides in his own personal exhibit at the museum, surrounded by artifacts which might be similar to the very kinds of goods that accompanied him on his original journey to the afterlife.

4. A Matter of Concealment

On April 25, 1986, a farmer in Sabine Parish took a good look down into the old well on his property in northwest Louisiana. He had not used the well in more than fifteen years but felt he needed to clean it out in order to have more water in the immediate region for his cattle. The blue, polyethylene plastic floating in the water quite a few feet down in the well was somewhat of a puzzle. Why in the world would such a large piece of plastic be down in the old well? The well was approximately thirty feet deep, but the plastic seemed to be lodged just about fifteen feet down into the well. The farmer found a long pole with a hook on the end and pulled the plastic toward the top of the well. As he did so, he was startled to see part of a human body looking up at him from the well below, lodged against the walls of the well. He called police.

In discussing the find with his father, the farmer's son disclosed that he had noticed the piece of plastic in the well just before Christmas in 1985 and had not really thought much about it, not even enough to mention it to his father.

After pumping approximately fifteen feet of water from the well, officers recovered part of a man's body. The man was dressed in a blue shirt, dark blue knit pants, and a blazer-type jacket. One blue sneaker was found in the well. An estimate of his height at the time he was recovered was approximately five feet, eight inches tall.

The 1986 autopsy indicated perimortem trauma to the body, which meant that something had happened to the man at or around the time of his death. Additionally, the autopsy recorded information about an old injury the man had experienced. Antemortem (before death) trauma to the unidentified man's left hip was severe. Number seven shot from an old shotgun injury was present in his pelvic region. He had at least twenty-eight visible shotgun pellets

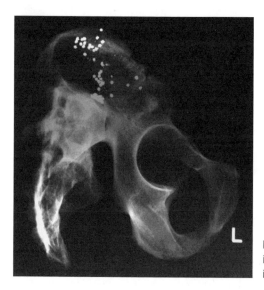

Figure 13. X-ray showing healed injuries with buckshot embedded in bone.

embedded in his left hip, and his left hip was fused to his sacrum (figure 13). The remodeling of the bone in the hip, which resulted in the fusion of the hip bone and the sacrum, was more than likely a result of the gunshot trauma. The trauma was well healed but may have given the man some problems when he walked.

By 2006, twenty years after the discovery of the man in the well, the case had been lost to public memory. One day that year Helen Bouzon and I were rummaging around in the attic at the Bossier Parish Pathology Center, looking for anything related to cases of unidentified persons in order to help build our comprehensive database for all of the unidentified and missing people in Louisiana. After Dr. McCormick of the center had died unexpectedly of a heart attack, his widow had given the FACES Lab permission to pull any and all bones from his lab. That particular day, we didn't come across the skeleton of the man in the well, or even any bone from the case, which we did not even know about at the time. But we did find a small paper bag with some numbers on it. The numbers linked the bag to holdings at the Bossier Center that were associated with Sabine Parish. We later discovered that authorities from

Sabine Parish had submitted the remains from the man found in the well to the Bossier Center but retrieved the remains shortly after McCormick's death. Within the small paper bag we discovered evidence, or artifacts, from the case (in archaeology, we sometimes refer to evidence as "artifacts"). Somehow, "artifacts" seemed appropriate in this case because we had been moving through the lab systematically (again, with the permission of Dr. McCormick's widow) and had been recovering items we felt to be significant for the database. The items in the small bag included a key ring with five keys, a folding brush/comb, a Snoopy nightlight, and a small pocket knife.

Within a matter of days after we found the small bag, the Bossier Center burned to the ground. The fire started by repair work in the attic, according to eyewitness accounts. Our plans to obtain the written records on the Sabine case, and on many others which we had retrieved from the lab, were thwarted. We had no written records on the significance of the material in the paper bag, or for that matter, many of the other cases we had retrieved from the lab in previous trips.

Archival research into the Sabine Parish case produced an article in the local paper about how the body was discovered in the well, but all we had to help solve the case was the small paper bag with the somewhat pitiful artifacts inside. A few weeks later, we contacted Mr. Ron Rivers, Sabine Parish coroner's investigator, who said he had some bones from the old case. He agreed to meet Helen and me in Zwolle, Louisiana, and hand over the skeletal remains to us for further analysis and for inclusion in our cold-case database. Those remains consisted of a skull and hip bones.

Our analysis for age of the man from the well was based on his auricular area and the pubic region of his hips. We concluded that he was somewhere between thirty and forty-five years of age. Measurements of his skull were plugged into the Fordisc database and reflected that, more than likely, he was a white male.

None of the bones provided to us by Ron Rivers was a long bone, typically what we use to determine height of an individual. We were uncertain as to how an estimate of height was determined originally, though it may have come from the length of the pants the man had been wearing. However, we deferred to the original height estimate of five feet, eight inches.

The skull of the victim reflected considerable dental restoration work. Minimally, he had a dental bridge from tooth #9 through tooth #13 (upper left central incisor through upper left second premolar). He also had a crown on his upper right, central incisor. Certain other teeth had been damaged, possibly perimortem, and whether they had repair work was unclear. Additionally, a number of teeth had been lost antemortem. Dental x-rays of a potential match for this person easily could be used to positively identify him.

One important resource for helping to identify cold cases often comes from retired detectives who worked the case or other investigators who were connected to it in some fashion. Mr. Ted DeLacerda, retired investigator for the DeSoto-Sabine District Attorney's Office, has followed this case for more than twenty years. He asked that the LSU FACES Laboratory complete a facial reconstruction on the case and publicize it for possible identification. We completed the facial reconstruction in 2008 (figure 14). The image was publicized in local and regional media, but as of 2013 this man remains unidentified. We believe he is a white male, between the ages of thirty and forty-five, who died at least six months or more prior to December 1985. His dental profile and the old shotgun injury to his hip are valuable identifiers. Someone must know of this man, must know of the life-threatening injury to his hip that he received, but which did not kill him at the time.

Previous efforts to retrieve a good DNA profile were unsuccessful with bone and teeth. Nuclear DNA results provided only a partial profile, while Y-STR analysis (only done on males) provided none. The Northeast Texas University laboratory is conducting mitochondrial DNA testing.

The man in the well was found in a cylinder-type grave, hidden from view for a considerable period of time, perhaps lost forever if the farmer had not decided to restore the old well. On still another

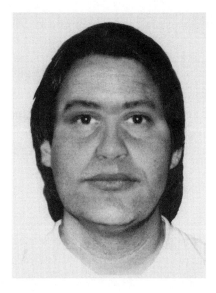

Figure 14. 3-D facial reconstruction of man found in well in 1986; image enhanced.

occasion, we encountered a case of a man in a cylinder-type tomb, though whoever disposed of his body used a different technique.

The landowner in Natchitoches Parish just off Highway 84 in northern Louisiana had ridden past the shallow stream on several occasions and had seen something that looked like metal protruding from the water's surface. He had not paid much attention to it until a dry spell in the region caused the metal to become more exposed. He recognized it as a sealed 55-gallon barrel and decided to take a closer look. However, the barrel was no longer sealed; part of the top had rusted away. When he got closer to the barrel, he saw what appeared to be bones inside; he immediately headed toward the nearest phone to call the sheriff's office.

On October 17, 2005, Ginny Listi and I were called to the Louisiana State Police Crime Laboratory to assist with the case. It became our case number 05-34 and was our first case of someone sealed in concrete in a barrel.

The barrel had been transported intact to the Louisiana State Police Crime Lab, and the lab's investigators had begun to extract the remains from the barrel. A small jackhammer was being used to separate the concrete from the bones. Over a period of several hours, we slowly removed all of the skeletal remains, hair, and clothing items from the barrel and transported the bones to our laboratory.

As we began to analyze the bones, we determined that more than likely they were the skeletal remains of a young black male, somewhere between the ages of eighteen and thirty. He was approximately five feet, eight inches tall, plus or minus an inch or two. Very little of his clothing items remained. No personal items, other than clothing, were found inside the barrel.

The young man had good dental work, though a few additional cavities had formed and had not been repaired. This usually suggests that some time had elapsed since his last visit to the dentist. Upon consultation with Dr. Ronald Carr—oral pathologist, retired faculty member of the LSU Dental School in New Orleans, and current member of the teaching faculty at the LSU Medical School in New Orleans—we learned about an unusual technique that was used to fill teeth. Dr. Carr noted that, in the 1950s, a Dr. Eastman was on the faculty at Loyola University in New Orleans. Dr. Eastman taught his students a filling technique referred to as the "bowtie" because it filled in the grooves on the occlusal, or chewing, surface of the tooth and looked something like a small bowtie. Dr. Carr noted that whoever performed the dental work on our unidentified man easily could have been trained by Dr. Eastman. Of course, over the years, probably hundreds, if not thousands, of dental students had been trained by Dr. Eastman. Therefore, though interesting, the only way in which that information might help would be to say that the young man may have at one time had dental work done in Louisiana, and, by extension, might have been from Louisiana.

These and other facts brought up the question as to how long the young man had been in the barrel. Since barrels can be archived or "saved" for great periods of time, we felt as though the barrel would not really provide us with a close enough time-table that could assist in getting the man identified. The small pieces of clothing that were left offered no evidence to suggest the year that they were made.

Figure 15. 3-D facial reconstruction of man found in barrel in 2005; image enhanced.

Finally, the decomposition was almost complete, and very little tissue was left on the body. Though a small amount of adipocere was still present in the concrete matrix, that soap-like substance, which is the result of hydrolysis of adipose, or fatty, body tissue, can last for hundreds of years. Lack of odor on the remains, however, did suggest that a minimum of several years had passed since the man was placed in the barrel.

In the end, we had no choice but to estimate that the young man may have been in the barrel for as little as two years and as many as twenty-five. Unfortunately, he remains unidentified. We have taken DNA samples which have been entered in the national DNA database (CODIS). Also, we have completed a three-dimensional facial reconstruction and Photoshop enhancement for him. Figure 15 represents what we believe he may have looked like in life.

One significant thing about this case makes me believe that it could be solved. The barrel alone was fairly heavy; the dead weight of a body is significant, especially an adult male. After he was put in the barrel, concrete was added to seal the barrel. Had whoever committed this crime anticipated that the barrel would sink to the bottom of the stream and stay there forever? Was the concrete put in the barrel by the side of the small stream? If not, one could suggest that the perpetrator might have had help moving the barrel and placing it in the water. Perhaps someone else has knowledge of the crime. When two people know something, sometimes one of them talks. It may be five years after the fact, or ten or more, but humans sometimes have a guilty conscience for the atrocities they perpetrate against their fellow humans. Let's hope someone does in this case. Though the man in the barrel was a case of deliberate concealment, another concealment case took a different twist and more than likely was not deliberate at all.

On a hot summer day in 2011, workmen were taking apart an interior wall in the second story of a nineteenth-century bank building in south Louisiana. They pulled back some wooden panels that had been placed over an old fireplace and began to disassemble the metal face piece. One of the workmen reached up inside the chimney where he saw some debris and began to pull it down to clean out the area. A human leg bone fell down on him. Of course, he screamed and called all the other carpenters to the area. The discovery would unravel a mystery more than twenty years in the making and leave another one unsolved.

The police department in the small town of Abbeville called me and asked if we could send a crew to assist with the recovery of what appeared to be a set of human remains wedged inside a historic building's chimney that had been closed from the roof for more than twenty years. Unfortunately, we had another call the same day from a different parish requesting help on a case where a dog had found the remains of a recently missing person in a shallow grave. I divided up our team, sending two assistants and graduate students to the burial site and taking one assistant and a graduate student with me to Abbeville.

When we arrived on the scene, I was intrigued by the architecture of the old building. A contractor stood nearby, hoping to have only a brief delay in his remodeling work. On the second floor we met with various detectives, some of whom had spent the night on the floor in sleeping bags to keep a watch over the site. I am always amazed at how dedicated law enforcement groups are when we ask them to just "secure everything until we get there." In all these years, we have never had a problem with anyone agreeing to do that.

My assistant, Helen Bouzon, and I evaluated the site. In a room directly adjacent to the room in which the remains were found, we noticed a twin fireplace that backed up to the one which held the victim's remains. We cautiously looked inside the fireplace for anything resembling human remains before we tackled the bone remains in the other room. The contractor explained that the second floor of the old building had not been used in almost fifty years and that the chimney itself had been closed off on the roof of the building at the top of the flue for at least twenty years.

Who was the victim, and why was he in the fireplace? National news media caught wind of the story, playing up the idea that someone other than Santa had tried to enter and exit a chimney. For the victim, entering the chimney was one thing; exiting it was something else entirely. Clearly unknown to him, the chimney in such older buildings and in many modern buildings narrows as it gets closer and closer to the actual fireplace opening itself. That is necessary for the chimney to "draw," or for the smoke from the fire to be drawn out of the chimney's smoke-stack and on out above the roof. Most likely, the victim was doomed the moment he began to slide down the chimney. Unless he exited the same way he entered, there would be no hope for him.

As we began to pull bones from inside the chimney, a few personal artifacts began to fall out also: a billfold with a driver's license in it, pieces of a belt, a shoe, bits and pieces of an old magazine. The skeletal remains were resting right at the top of the fireplace on the metal that was part of the surround that encircled the fireplace. That metal grate was no more than six inches wide. No one could exit that chimney through the fireplace opening.

As usual in a field recovery, we created a plan view, or sketch, of the remains as we saw them on the floor in front of the fireplace and as they rested in the chimney. I stuck gloved hands up inside the chimney and began to remove the bones one by one. We had recovered most all of the bones that were visible except for the cranium. It was stuck and would not come through the small opening. Police officers took crowbars and began to pull away the brick at the top of the fireplace in order for us to get to the cranium. It only required a couple of layers of brick and the cranium was exposed. I gently lifted it out of the chimney and recognized immediately that it was the skull of a young white male and, more than likely, the very one whose driver's license had fallen into the fireplace earlier.

We gathered all remains together, made sure there were no others there, and put them in bags to take back to the laboratory at LSU.

For the next couple of weeks, we went over the bones carefully, first x-raying them to look for any evidence of perimortem trauma, that is, injury at or near the time of death. We found none. We then sampled the remains for DNA testing to make certain the skeletal remains matched the identity of the person on the driver's license. The family of the license holder had provided buccal swabs from their cheeks to compare to the DNA from the young man's bones. The identity was confirmed. It was the same young man whose license was also found in the chimney.

The biggest mystery of all is why the young man was in the chimney in the first place. He had been in the military and had come home. Following some problems with the law, he was scheduled for a court hearing at the time he disappeared. Many people suspected he had just run away. However, he had a small son whom he loved dearly. His family felt he would not have disappeared and never returned to see his son. It was out of character for him. Why did he climb into the chimney? Was he trying to hide? Did he have something else in mind? We will probably never know.

We do believe the man entered the chimney deliberately, because there was no evidence on his remains of any kind of violence. Once inside the chimney, he must have become stuck and was unable to get out the way he got in. The harder he worked at getting out, the faster he was stuck. Also, it is unlikely that anyone could have heard his cries for help since they would have been muffled by the chimney itself. The fireplace on the second floor of the historic building was not being used because that floor had been closed off for years. The chimney became his tomb.

Some years later, the original chimney opening on top of the building was covered over, perhaps because maintenance people may have thought it would prevent rain from getting into the building or would prevent small animals such as birds or squirrels from nesting inside the chimney. When the chimney opening on the roof was sealed shut in the late 1980s, all chances of the young man's body being discovered were lost. He remained there until 2011 when the remodeling job on the second floor required removal of the chimney. If the bank building had not been renovated, more than likely the young man would have been there another 100 years or more before the building was demolished or fell down. By then, all memory of him and much of the evidence may have been gone. His concealment in the chimney and his inaudible calls for help must have made death a terrible ordeal. He has finally been given a place of rest by his family.

5. The Power of Tattoos

The driver of the eighteen-wheeler had just finished eating a late dinner right after midnight on that hot July night in 1990 in Hammond, Louisiana. He was heading for his truck parked close to the highway when something caught his eye. As he edged closer to what looked like a pile of rags, he almost lost his dinner. Lying there in the parking lot of the popular truck stop was what was left of a man's body. His body was heavily damaged with face, viscera, and part of one leg missing.

Several days after the man was found, I was called by the coroner's office in Tangipahoa Parish and asked to help provide some kind of profile on the man. It was thought he may have fallen from the belly of one of the large transport trucks that carry various goods all across the United States. The Hammond truck stop was a favorite place for the truckers to stop for food and gas. The man had no identification on him, and no one in the area had been reported missing.

At the time, I typically worked alone except with the assistance of a graduate or undergraduate student here or there who wanted experience in forensic anthropology. No funding was available for graduate assistants, but I rounded up two students who agreed to help with the case. This particular case required that we visit a funeral home some miles out of the city where the body had been taken. When we arrived, we were shown to a small building behind the funeral home where we found the body in a body bag with hundreds of insects flying around. Since decomposition had become fairly advanced, the body had to be isolated from others inside the funeral home.

Authorities had indicated that the man was covered with tattoos that might possibly help to identify him. One of the students who accompanied me was Jim McLean, an artist. Ultimately, Jim's help would prove to be especially important in this case.

ON Back
from just under scapula
to lumbar region

Figure 16. Unusual tattoo, found on back of man, which aided in identification.

When we opened the door to the building that day, hundreds of flies scattered immediately but returned just as quickly. Working as fast as we could, we recovered the hips and a long bone in order to try to determine the man's age and height. Since the face and skull were heavily damaged, we knew that ancestry, or race, would be difficult to assess. However, hair texture and other features suggested that the man might be a white individual.

Jim sketched the numerous tattoos across the body while the other student and I extracted the hips and femur. We returned to the lab and were told that, unless we were able to identify the man quickly, he would be buried by the funeral home as an unknown. Fingerprints had been taken, but no matches were found.

We began to evaluate the tattoos and saw a clear pattern. The name "Jim" was tattooed on one arm. Also, the tattoos included many nautical images: an anchor, a ship which looked like an ancient schooner, a female figure who appeared to be wearing a hula skirt, and what might have been "HMS" on his arm with "Navy" below it. A very large tattoo of a female's face with flowing hair covered much of his back. That image, to me, was reminiscent of the sirens who called to Jason and the Argonauts in ancient myths and clearly was unique to this individual (figure 16).

In the years to follow, whenever I gave presentations at law enforcement workshops across the state and the Southeast, I showed the pictures of the tattoos to officers. No one had anyone reported missing who fit the man's description. Eventually, once the database got started, we took a DNA sample from his femur and entered it into the national CODIS database, hoping for a cold-case hit. Nothing came up.

The nautical tattoos made me think that perhaps the unidentified man had been in the Navy or the merchant marines, but the fingerprints taken earlier had not been matched to anyone. Since he had what might have been "HMS" tattooed on one arm, we even thought that perhaps he was in "Her Majesty's Service" for Great Britain. In fact, by 2010, we had decided to try contacting Canada's Royal Mounted Police on the outside chance that he had made his way down south from Canada. Before we could do that, something quite extraordinary occurred.

In the spring of 2010, in Biloxi, Mississippi, I was giving a presentation at a mass disaster conference when Fran Wheatley, a friend of mine whom I had not seen in years and who was then working in Mississippi, came over to catch up on old times. Fran was especially interested in our database and asked several questions regarding it. She went on her way, and we parted with promises to stay in touch more often. A short time later, a woman called Fran with an important question. Did Mississippi have a database for unidentified and/or missing people? It seems that her uncle had last been heard from almost twenty years prior when he was in Mississippi and on his way to Texas to see family members. Fran explained to the woman that Mississippi did not have such a database but that Louisiana did and that she should look at our database and contact us if any case in the database looked promising.

Janice Carroll contacted us soon thereafter and told us that our case 90-09 might be her uncle, James Nelson, and that she and her mom, Gay Denton, James Nelson's sister, recently had begun to search the web to try to find out if anyone knew what happened to their brother and uncle all those years ago. Multiple success stories highlighted on national television about missing people had compelled them to do so. When Janice searched our website, she was instantly drawn to case 90-09.

Naturally, we hoped that our case was indeed her uncle. Not only would it give the family some peace of mind to find him, it would mean that the database was successful in doing what we wanted it to do—provide information that might get some of the people in it identified.

Though James Nelson was known by family members to have been in the Navy, we were especially excited when Janice Carroll said that her aunt, Alice Langley, told her that her Uncle Jim had "some kind of big tattoo on his back." Alice recognized the tattoo when Janice showed her a picture of it.

Helen Bouzon and I visited back and forth with the family. We received DNA samples from them and consequently were able to name the man whose identity had initially appeared so easy to solve but had eluded us for almost twenty years. His body had been buried as a John Doe in the parish cemetery. The bones from which we had extracted the DNA were curated in our laboratory. The Tangipahoa Parish coroner's office collected all remains and sent them to Mr. Nelson's family in 2010.

The question is always, "What happened to him?" Of course, we will never know for certain, but two options seem possible. Alice Langley repeated her earlier statement that the night Jim disappeared he was in Mississippi and was headed to Texas to see family members. Both Alice Langley and Gay Denton noted that their brother loved to travel, loved to visit different places, and was "a lover of life, a lover of the open road." They both agreed that he often hitchhiked, typically traveling from Florida to Texas and back to visit relatives. The family last heard from him when he was in Pascagoula, Mississippi, and began immediately to look for him, contacting law enforcement agencies all across the South when they could not find him. Somehow, his case, like others, slipped through the cracks.

He may have been hit by one of the eighteen-wheelers that travel the roads late at night. If this happened while he was still in Mississippi, he could have been dragged as many as a hundred miles. If his body was lodged under a large truck, that might explain the damage. The driver might not even have known that he hit him. Mr. Nelson's body might have been caught under the truck and fell out later at the truck stop when the driver took a break. Another possible scenario is that he tried to hitch a ride under the belly of a truck, in one of the large wheel wells that typically hold the oversized tires that truckers carry as spares. Though this seems unlikely, it could explain the extensive damage to only part of his body. We will never be able to recapture the events that led to his presence in the truck-stop parking lot, but the family knows now where their brother and uncle is, in a grave of their choice.

Many people (including those of us who "came of age" in the 1960s) seem to have at least one tattoo these days. As in the Hammond truck-stop case, these tattoos remain a reliable way of getting someone identified, or at least providing what we call a putative, or preliminary identification. Oftentimes, a person will have at least one self-identifying tattoo on his or her body, whether it is the person's name or nickname, the name of a loved one, or the name of a former girlfriend or boyfriend.

In terms of preservation of tattoos on a decomposing body, if the skin has not totally decomposed, forensic anthropologists might find tattoos that were missed during the initial autopsy. One such case was that of a young female who was a homicide victim. The perpetrator had also set her body on fire, but someone noticed the body and put out the fire before too much damage had occurred. Many of her more than twenty tattoos had been documented at autopsy, but we were able to find several others that had been missed. However, even with a facial reconstruction, we were still unable to get her identified. The local police published a drawing in the newspaper which included all of the tattoos we had documented (figure 17). Still, nothing led to her identification.

Finally, a family member from out of state contacted the local police in New Orleans and told them that her sister had been in

Figure 17. Tattoos on homicide victim, which assisted with identification.

New Orleans and had not returned home. The family member wanted to know if any young, black females' bodies had been found lately. The detective who spoke to the young woman explored the case of the woman with all of the tattoos. She noted that her sister had multiple tattoos; she gave the sister's name, "Aeisha." One of the tattoos on the young unidentified, black female was "Aeisha." DNA provided positive identification. With the help of the tattoos, it took only a few months before the case was resolved. We were fortunate on at least two counts: one, that the body was out in the open and was found before the tattoos had deteriorated to the point where they could not be distinguished clearly; and two, that the family member knew something about the last known whereabouts of the young woman and called law enforcement in that area before a great deal of time had elapsed. Unfortunately, the perpetrator has not been found.

Often, what are referred to as "jail house tattoos" can also assist law enforcement agencies in helping to determine whether someone might have been in prison at one time. Usually, they are monotone, typically a bluish/black color and sometimes appear to be fairly primitive. However, in recent years, many of these jailhouse tattoo artists have become quite adept at their work and have produced tattoos that are very professional in appearance. These tattoos are hard to trace.

Even a single tattoo can lead to a person's identity. In one case many years ago, a young man died accidentally and was found on the river bank several months after he had disappeared. After the autopsy was performed, the remains were sent to us for further processing since he could not be identified. We began to examine his body, though his skin was desiccated, or somewhat mummified. After lying out on the riverbank for what had been estimated to be several months, only a few small sections of his body still had skin. On his arm, we found a small, single-word tattoo: "Black." The coroner's investigator thought it could be specific to the young man. He went to the home of a missing man and asked his mother, "Did your son have any tattoos on his body?" She told the investigating officer that he had one tattoo, that his nickname was "Black," and that the tattoo was on his right forearm near the elbow. It matched what we had found.

6. The Power of Fingerprints

He was known in the small town of Eunice, Louisiana, in St. Landry Parish, as "the bicycle man." He had appeared a few months prior and often could be seen riding his bicycle throughout the area. Sometimes he pulled a small cart on wheels behind the bike. He bothered no one and seemed quite friendly, but a loner to most. One evening in late spring near dusk, 2005, he was struck accidentally by a car as he rode along a highway near town. The woman who hit him was driving at a normal speed but had not seen him on the road. He died at the scene. No one knew for certain who he was. He lay in a parish coroner's office for almost two months and still had no name. In a conversation with an investigator from Lafayette Parish one day at a conference, I found out about the case. Since it had been months since he was discovered, his body was about to be cremated as an unidentified person. I quickly called the coroner of St. Landry and told him we would be happy to take the body and try to get him identified, to please not cremate the victim. Unfortunately, in the past, in our state and in many states, bodies that could not be identified were cremated within a relatively brief period of time after discovery. This was due in no small part to lack of storage space in most morgues.

The coroner's office submitted the body to us, and we began the task of creating a profile on him and trying to get him identified. He was an older white male, we thought, somewhere between the ages of fifty and sixty-five. He had a copious amount of antemortem trauma across his skeleton which included what might have been a healed, broken shoulder and a healed, broken leg. Both of those regions had previously been sutured, and sutures were still visible near and around the injury sites. The injuries suggested that he had a medical history somewhere, perhaps from other bicycle accidents.

Also, he had incurred multiple perimortem injuries from the fatal bike accident.

His fingerprints had been submitted locally, but they had not resulted in a positive identification. We felt that with our profile and a little extra inquiry he at least had a chance to be identified, a chance he never would have had if he had been cremated as previously planned.

Papers within the man's backpack that accompanied his body suggested a name. A Walmart ticket in the bag was traced to a local store where he was caught on tape purchasing supplies. With a potential name, we went to the Louisiana State Police Crime Laboratory and asked for assistance from their amazing fingerprint experts. They ran the prints and asked for the inquiry to include military prints. They called a day or so later and said, "Mary, we have a match. Your victim is a Vietnam veteran who was sixty-five years old when he died." I thought our quest was over. It was not. We were in a dilemma because we could not find his family. Generally, we do not act as detectives in trying to seek out family members, though I have done so in the past in order to obtain information on previous medical records for positive identification purposes. This was different. We knew who the man was; we just did not know where his family was.

In a last-ditch effort to associate his name with a family, I contacted an old friend in the FBI, and she was able to provide information on his family in a northwestern state. He had five children, all of whom loved him very much and had been concerned because they had been unable to locate him for several years. It seems that he had gotten a divorce from their mother and had decided to sell his home and see the country on his bicycle. They had last heard from him when he left home, saying he was heading for Florida to help with hurricane victims. If not for the fingerprints, we probably never would have identified him and located his family. They were most grateful for our help. If we had not heard about this case simply through luck, the victim would have been cremated and more than likely would never have been identified. His family never would have known the whereabouts of their loved one. The family was very grateful for our help and thought that he would have liked for his remains to be donated to science since he always wanted to help people. They donated his skeleton to our laboratory. Authorities never found the small cart he often pulled behind his bike.

Another case where fingerprints proved essential in the identification process, but where it took years to solve the identity of the young teenager, was first highlighted in my book <u>Trail of Bones,</u> published in 2005. That homicide victim was a young white male who had been found in the woods in 1979 in St. Helena Parish near Greensburg, Louisiana. In July 2000, at the request of Detective Dennis Stewart of the Louisiana State Police, we had exhumed the teenager's remains because someone had contacted Dennis about the case, thinking that the teenager's description fit that of the missing son of a family in the northeastern part of the country. At the time of the exhumation, we had great expectations that the young man might be the missing son and that we could help to solve his identity. We conducted our usual analysis on his case once we exhumed him and confirmed that he was a young white male between the ages of fourteen and sixteen. We extracted a DNA sample from one bone and a tooth but were concerned that a full DNA profile might not be obtained since the remains had been buried for twenty-two years. However, the DNA laboratory was able to get a full DNA profile from the tooth.

The DNA comparison showed that the young man was not the missing son. That was greatly disappointing for us and for Detective Stewart, who had been trying for years to get the young man identified. Enter IAFIS, the most comprehensive and powerful fingerprint database in the world, the same database used to identify the man on the bicycle. IAFIS is the acronym for the FBI's "Integrated Automated Fingerprint Identification System" which was not established until 1999, twenty years after the teenager was found in 1979. When the boy's body was first discovered, the pathologist who performed the autopsy determined that he had been dead less than two days. Fingerprints were easy to recover. Authorities had run those fingerprints through their local database but had been unable at the time to compare them to various missing-persons cases across the country. In 1979, in order to run them on a national basis, cases were sent to the FBI, and each case submitted could take weeks or months to process. Even then, authorities might reach a dead end, as they did in the teenager's case. In 2008, Detective Stewart wanted to try one more time to submit the young teenager's prints. He sent them through IAFIS, well established by that time, and he received an immediate hit. That hit was due to the fact that the young man had experienced a brief, nonviolent encounter with a law enforcement agency in Texas a short time before he was found dead in Louisiana in 1979. At the time, he was fingerprinted. Those fingerprints ultimately were entered into IAFIS. Almost thirty years after the teenager disappeared, Daniel Wayne Dewey's family gained some peace of mind.

A similar case was that of an older white male who was found in the woods in St. James Parish in 1994. He had been dead for one to two weeks when he was found. He had multiple tattoos across his body, including a bluebird over each nipple on his chest. He also had a tattoo that said "mother" and one that read "B-4-Lynn" that was part of a separated heart. One assumed that Lynn had broken his heart some time in the past. We completed a facial reconstruction on the man and posted it on our website for unidentified and missing people. No one came forward in all that time. In 2008, a detective in the St. James Parish Sheriff's Office decided to submit the man's fingerprints to IAFIS, which was not available in 1994 when the man was found. There was an immediate hit on the man. The man found in the woods in 1994 was identified in 2008. However, it took FACES Lab Research Associate Helen Bouzon until 2012 to find his family member. Previous efforts by both law enforcement personnel and the local sheriff's office had been unsuccessful. The family generously donated his remains to the FACES Laboratory for use in teaching.

The national CODIS database for DNA identifications is a powerful database and, often, is the database that receives the most attention, but fingerprints should not be ignored as a way to identify cold cases. The three previous examples point to the power of fingerprints and how the tenacity of some agencies plays a major role in getting old cases solved.

7. A Son's Transgression

As we were about to enter the private home where a set of human remains had been found in an upstairs bedroom, the neighbor walked over to me and said, "Yeah, we've been seeing a bunch of flies around that second-story window for quite some time and wondered what that was about." I looked at him in disbelief. Flies around a window always, always mean there is something dead inside!

We had received a phone call that day from the Jefferson Parish Sheriff's Office and the Coroner's Office. A man's body had been found in the upstairs bedroom of a home in Metairie, Louisiana, and authorities were asking for our help in removing the body and analyzing the remains. When I asked why they felt our assistance was necessary, they explained that they believed that the remains were those of an elderly gentleman who may have been dead for more than a year and who had been kept in the house for all of that time. I asked how long had it been since the house had been occupied. They replied that it was still occupied by the son and grandson of the dead man. In fact, they suggested that the elderly gentleman may have been in the bedroom since soon after Katrina in 2005. Hurricane Katrina had devastated the Gulf Coast in August of 2005. Its immediate damage and aftermath were especially hard for New Orleans because levees broke in canals there and flooded multiple areas of the city. The city was shut down for months and in 2013 has yet to fully recover from the storm.

I gathered supplies and assistants, and we headed southeast toward New Orleans. The Big Easy and its immediate communities encompass two parishes, Orleans and Jefferson. Both parishes have sections on the east and west sides of the Mississippi River. The subdivision where we were headed was a middle-class neighborhood with well-manicured lawns.

When we arrived on the scene, the investigators gave us a few preliminary details. They also restated how a neighbor had noted flies at the upstairs window of the dead man's house off and on over the previous months. Again, flies do not normally hang out around windows. Their presence anywhere near a private dwelling should sound an alarm. They are looking for places to lay their eggs, and those places are decomposing tissue, human or otherwise.

The authorities had been called to the house originally when the daughter of the elderly gentlemen had contacted them, saying that her brother refused to allow her to see their father. For more than a year, he had told her that the eighty-two-year-old man was either asleep, not feeling well, or not at home when she had tried to visit. When authorities arrived, the son, fifty-five years old, did not want to let them in at first, but they insisted. When they entered the house, the stench was overpowering. They searched the house, discovered the elderly gentleman in his bed, and called the coroner. The decision was made to call us in.

When we opened the front door of the house and walked inside, the smell was almost overwhelming. We followed the investigators up the stairs and toward a bedroom on the left at the head of the stairs. There on a mattress, partially wrapped in a blanket were the skeletonized remains of an individual. We immediately began to photograph the remains, quickly create a sketch, or plan view, of how he was laid out, and remove him from the room. We had already explained to the agencies that once we removed him he would go to our laboratory. They were in complete agreement.

The window and the room were covered with dead flies. Lifeless larvae, or maggots, were found throughout the area. The ceiling in the bedroom drooped in the middle, a consequence, someone said, of Katrina damage to the roof. We asked where the son was and were told that he was in jail. We asked where the grandson was, a thirty-three-year-old man with learning disabilities. They told us he was with family.

What we hoped would be a case of death by natural causes turned out to be something entirely different. Once again, I would find myself in a court of law testifying about perimortem trauma—injury found on a skeleton that occurred at or around the time of death.

We finished taking photographs of the remains and documenting every detail we could while the body was still in place. Then, we carefully wrapped sheets around the body and placed it in a body bag. After leaving the house, where reporters were gathered outside, we placed the remains in our vehicle and transported them to our laboratory in Baton Rouge.

When we started our analysis in the lab a day later, we began to document signs of perimortem trauma throughout the skeleton: several broken ribs, a broken hyoid (the little bone that helps to anchor the tongue in place), a broken toe, a broken finger, all on a man who was over eighty years old. In the case of the ribs, we also saw evidence of old breaks that were in the process of healing, suggesting more than one episode of injury.

According to police, the son explained that the elderly gentleman had fallen down the stairs and that he, the son, had picked him up. He said he then put him back in bed and sort of fell on him when he put him into the bed, perhaps injuring him even more at the time. When I heard this, I knew that I would be looking into the eyes of the son in a court of law in the future because something just did not sound right about his explanation.

Once we had completed our analysis of the different injuries on the man's bones, we contacted the coroner's office and met with the pathologist to show her what we had found. Dr. Karen Ross, the forensic pathologist, noted that, when someone falls down a set of stairs, typically it is a series of short falls, not like what you see on television. We all expected subpoenas in the next few months, and we were right. The case was going to trial.

If anyone tells you they are not nervous about testifying in court, I suggest that person may not be telling the whole truth. Court looks very different from the other side of the bench. Anyone with a drop of integrity wants to tell the truth, the whole truth, and nothing but the truth. As forensic anthropologists, our truth comes from the evidence we see on the bones. We study bones. We understand growth and development. We understand the aging process. We understand the dynamics of injury to the bone. And we give an opinion on what we see in the individual bones of a person. That opinion takes into consideration all of our years of training, and, just as important, all of our many years of experience working with thousands and thousands of human bones.

In court that day, the prosecutor had asked me to bring a plastic skeleton that demonstrated the areas across the body that had been injured. I complied. I had put a small marker on each of the bones where trauma had been found, and I stood the skeleton before the jury. I remember being somewhat nervous, but I felt comfortable with explaining the trauma to the jury. It was as though I was back in class with my students. The jury was very attentive, as I have observed most jurors to be over the last twenty-five years. By the time I had finished a couple of hours later, I had described all of the injuries we had found.

On cross-examination, the defense attorney asked if in my opinion the injuries the elderly man had received could be a result of osteoporosis and a fall of less than one foot from his bed onto a small trunk used as a night table. I replied that, in my opinion, I did not believe that could happen. Not only were the injuries fairly extensive, they were also widespread. What I could not do was tell the jury how they occurred; that I did not know.

Dr. Karen Ross also testified in court to the trauma that we found on the bones. She noted that the injuries—to the ribs, to the toe, to the finger, to the hyoid—in her opinion represented injuries that could have led to the death of the man, especially if he had not had proper medical care. No evidence existed that showed he had been seen by a medical doctor.

Subsequently, the defense attorney introduced a medical doctor who said that the victim had osteoporosis and that a person with osteoporosis could possibly break all of those bones by a short fall of twelve inches or so onto a trunk that, allegedly, was near the bed.

In the end, the jury could not convict the man of second-degree murder, a conviction in Louisiana that would have resulted in life in prison without benefit of parole. However, the members of the jury did believe that the elderly man's fifty-five-year-old son contributed to his death, whether accidentally or on purpose. They found him guilty of manslaughter, a crime that can carry a fairly stiff prison sentence. In this instance, the judge sentenced the man to twenty years in prison. He will be an old man himself when he is released. Let's hope that he is treated a little more kindly than his father was.

As more and more American citizens age, it is extremely important for both forensic pathologists and forensic anthropologists to be aware of the injuries that can suggest elder abuse—especially by caregivers, whether family members, medical care providers, nursing home employees, or anyone else who has access to that person. In recent years, studies have indicated that elder abuse is on the rise, and, like child abuse, appropriate inquiry is required when an elderly person dies and foul play is suspected.

8. Man Overboard

The Ross Barnett Reservoir near Brandon, Mississippi, is a large artificial body of water surrounded by expensive homes, condominiums, and apartment complexes. On April 28, 2011, in the vicinity of a row of apartments, a man looked out across the water and saw what he thought was a body floating in the water. He immediately called authorities. The subsequent autopsy report noted that the white male was somewhere between fifty and sixty-five years of age, more than likely weighed around two hundred pounds, and was wearing shorts and a T-shirt. He had died by drowning. For almost five months, investigators Chris Barnes and Tim Lawless worked the case, trying to get the man identified. Their search took them to all dwellings around the reservoir, where they asked everyone who lived there if they knew of a neighbor who was missing or perhaps someone who was visiting the area and who had not been seen lately.

A few days before the body was found, someone had discovered an abandoned kayak quite a distance away from the body, but authorities had no idea whether the kayak was associated with the man.

In May 2011, authorities had a conversation with a potential witness who told them that he had encountered an older, white male in a kayak one evening in late April and had given him a small flashlight. Though the investigators were grateful for the information, it still did not lead to a positive identification of the drowning victim. Authorities were completely frustrated with their efforts. They even tried to get an image of the man out to the public to see if anyone recognized him. No one came forward to suggest that he or she knew who the victim was.

Having heard about our work at the LSU FACES Laboratory, and especially the success of our imaging specialist, Eileen Barrow, they called me in September, approximately four and one half months

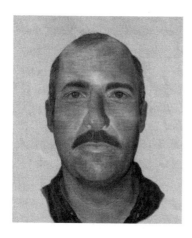

Figure 18. Facial reconstruction of man found in Ross Barnett Reservoir; image enhanced.

after the man's body had been discovered, to ask if the FACES Laboratory would assist them in trying to get the man identified. Of course, we agreed. On September 13, 2011, the cranium, mandible, and first two cervical vertebrae of the unidentified man were submitted to us by the Rankin County Sheriff's Office in Brandon, Mississippi.

Figure 18 is the image Eileen Barrow completed and we submitted to Rankin County. A day after the image was placed in the local newspaper, someone called investigators with their first clear lead. The caller said that he felt that the man in the facial reconstruction was Mr. Larry Daugherty. Subsequently, dental records were used to identify the man positively as Mr. Daugherty (figure 19). Where was the disconnect in this case? It was simple. Mr. Daugherty's family noted he had recently retired to the reservoir area, and they felt that few in the area knew him. He had not had time to make new friends. They also noted that he had a kayak and loved to take it out into the reservoir. However—and this was most important—he had informed his family back in April, only a short time before his body was found, that he had met a lovely woman on the web and that he would be taking a trip out of the country with her. The family

Figure 19. Larry Daugherty.

simply thought that he had left the country and was having such a good time with his new friend that he had failed to contact them and let them know where he was. After a few months, however, they had become concerned about not hearing from him for so long.

One of the keys to resolving this case was certainly the tenacity of detectives Barnes and Lawless. They did not want to let it go. Another was the publicity for the image created by the FACES Laboratory. The Daughtery case was not the first to be resolved by the public airing of an image created by an agency—in this case, ours. Law enforcement authorities may have an imaging specialist create a likeness of an unidentified person, but if that image is not publicized several times, the positive identification of that person may never happen. Publicize, publicize, publicize. It is not always about the image looking exactly like the person, though in Mr. Daughtery's case, we were fortunate that it did. The important thing is to keep the image before the public's eye so that it will attract the attention of someone who knows that person and says to himself or herself, "He looks familiar to me." And then, of course, the person who says that must follow through by calling authorities on the off chance that it could be that person. Many of our cases have been solved for that very reason. The image was not always spot on, but the description of events, the timing of the case, and other factors suggested to the viewers, to the readers, to the observers, something familiar. In the end, the public's attention to the details often helps to resolve a case.

9. A Child from the Past

The cemetery worker was somewhat surprised at what lay before him as he dismantled the old burial vault. Certain vaults in historic St. Joseph's Cemetery in Thibodaux, Louisiana, were in the process of being refurbished, while others were being dismantled. During the dismantlement of one of the vaults, the cemetery worker discovered an underground component to the vault with a small cast iron coffin resting inside. The coffin had a glass viewing plate at the head end, and fairly well-preserved human remains were visible to the cemetery personnel.

The vault was one of two owned by the Toups family. Descendants had decided to place the deceased from the two vaults within just one vault in order to donate the other vault to the Catholic Diocese of Houma-Thibodaux. The identity of the person in the small coffin was unknown to the descendants.

Knowing of our interest in historic graves and what they could tell us about the recent past, Mr. George Cook, director and administrator of the diocese's Office of Cemeteries, contacted me and asked if we would be interested in looking at the remains of what he thought was a child inside the cast iron coffin. Of course, I was interested. Mr. Cook then contacted the Toups family representative, Mrs. Merlin Simek, about the possibility of allowing the LSU FACES Laboratory the opportunity to study the remains. In so doing, Mr. Cook relayed to Mrs. Simek that we might possibly provide a name for the child. Mrs. Simek and other family members graciously agreed.

After an initial meeting with Mrs. Simek and her family in 2008, we assembled a team of experts to assist with the project and invited them and the Toups family descendants to the opening of the coffin. We wanted the family to be comfortable with the analysis and to witness the care with which we handle such cases. We do not take lightly the responsibility of removing someone from a final resting place and analyzing his or her remains. The cast iron coffin was destined to be opened, whether we did it or not. The remains would have been removed and slipped in beside other remains in the standing tomb. The coffin would have been destroyed. Any information about who the child was or when he or she died would have been lost forever.

Our team of experts included a forensic odontologist (Dr. Robert Barsley of the LSU Dental School in New Orleans), a chemist (Dr. Frank Fronzcek of LSU), a horticulturalist (Dr. Jeff Kuehny of LSU), a forensic pathologist (Dr. Karen Ross, at the time with the Jefferson Parish Coroner's Office), a textile expert (Dr. Jenna Kutruff of LSU), a bioarchaeologist (Mr. Hampton Peele of LSU), a geologist (Mr. Rick Young of LSU), the FACES team of forensic anthropologists, imaging specialists, and bioarchaeologists, and finally, multiple graduate students in anthropology and human ecology.

When Mrs. Simek arrived at the FACES Laboratory for the coffin's opening and initial assessment, she carried with her a sealed envelope that contained information about a possible identity for the child in the coffin. She had found the document after our initial meeting. We asked her not to reveal the information inside the envelope until after our preliminary analysis.

The opening of such a coffin is always a time of tense anticipation. We had worked on multiple other such coffins in the past and had learned that one never knows what to expect in such a situation, anything from well-preserved remains to simply dried-out bones. However, the glass viewing plate at the head location revealed that we definitely would find some intact remains and most likely at least some clothing in good condition. The glass viewing plate had been covered by a metal cover with a hinge to allow the bereaved to view the face of their loved one during the traditional wake. Cemetery workers assured us that the metal cover had been intact when the coffin was first discovered but was misplaced subsequently in the initial recovery process. Because of the viewing plate, we knew before we started that the body inside the coffin

Figure 20. Superior view of nineteenth-century cast-iron coffin.

Figure 21. Lateral view of nineteenth-century cast-iron coffin.

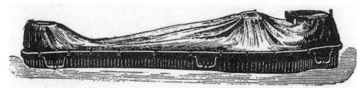

Figure 22. Catalog image of Fisk metal coffin.

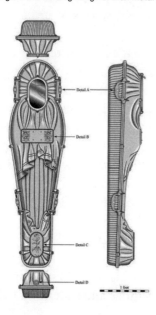

Figure 23. Drawing of historic burial coffin.

looked fairly well preserved, that a bonnet of some kind was over the head, and that a small wreath of artificial flowers most likely had been placed over the head but had slipped down over the face. What we did not know was how well the rest of the body or other artifacts would be preserved.

The coffin was intriguing. It reminded me immediately of others I had recorded from mid-nineteenth-century burials on which I had worked in the past. It was made of cast iron and had what often is referred to as a mummy's shape (figures 20 and 21). It appeared to be a Fisk coffin, which was patented in the mid-1800s, was broad at the shoulder region, and narrowed down at the feet. Additionally, the metal cover was molded in such a way as to represent folds of cloth cascading down the length of the coffin. It had two handles on each side. Except for the two handles, the coffin was a ringer for the original one patented by Almond D. Fisk in 1848 (figure 22). The "Fisk burial case," as it often was called, provided an air-tight environment for human remains. The prototype for the Fisk burial case showed three handles on each side, but that was an adult's coffin. This clearly was that of a child (figure 23).

Hampton Peele was unable to remove the screws securing the coffin lid in place since they had rusted to the rest of the coffin. Instead, he ground them off with a grinder, and we lifted the top from the coffin. Inside were multiple surprises.

As expected, the remains were those of a small child, most likely female, judging by the clothing that consisted of the bonnet we had seen through the viewing glass, a dress, stockings, and shoes. We were all drawn to the shoes. They were perfectly preserved, as though they had been placed inside the coffin only a few days earlier (figure 24). The shoes were new and had gold-stamped designs on them. The designs included cherubs, cornucopias, and floral motifs. More than likely, they were special burial shoes.

As in any forensic case, the first thing we planned to do was x-ray the remains. However, first we had to get them out of the coffin. The coffin was partially filled with a black liquid substance, more than likely a combination of body fluids and water that had

Figure 24. Shoes with gold design.

entered the coffin at some point. Before we lifted the body from the coffin, we had another surprise: botanical remains. Plants of varying species and sizes were found throughout the coffin. According to Dr. Jeff Kuehy, LSU botanist, they consisted of heliotrope, gardenia, scented geranium, rose, eastern red cedar, and thyme. Most surprising of all, they were well preserved and many of them still retained their green color! We had never seen such good preservation of plants in historic burials. Roses were the most abundant and were found near the head, at the right elbow, and between the lower legs. A scented geranium branch was in the right hand. All of these plants have strong fragrances and, historically, were placed in burials to reduce decomposition odors. Figure 25 is Eastern Red Cedar; figure 26 is thyme.

The full-body x-rays of the child revealed that her clothing had many pins in it, perhaps to give the appearance of a good fit. The x-rays also revealed information important to the age of the child. Children are born with approximately 450 centers of bone growth that ultimately fuse into the 206 bones of an adult skeleton. Various bones complete their growth at different times during an individual's life. Once a particular bone has completed its growth, the end of that bone, or epiphysis, fuses to the rest of the bone. Of course, the child's epiphyses were wide open on many of her bones.

Figure 25. Eastern cedar found in coffin.

Figure 26. Thyme found in coffin.

Her dental development gave us added information about her profile. According to Dr. Robert Barsley, the forensic odontologist, her deciduous molars (often called baby molars) were fully formed, and the partially developed crowns of her permanent premolars (bicuspids) were present. To Dr. Barsley, this suggested an age range for the child from three and one-half years old to seven years, with his best estimate at five years, plus or minus four months. Her long-bone development suggested an age range of four to four and one-half years. Though long-bone growth is susceptible to the quality and proportion of food intake, disease processes, parasitic influence, and other circumstances, the child in the coffin had long-bone development suggestive of a child older than three years.

Further evaluation of the health of the child revealed two minor cavities in her teeth and small pinpoint porosities in several areas across her skull. The porosities in the skull might indicate an iron-poor diet or inability to absorb iron, perhaps due to parasites. These porosities often are found in ancient and modern skeletal remains. Added to these general health indicators was the possible Harris Line in one of her distal tibiae. Viewed via an x-ray of the long bones (the femur, tibia, radius, ulna, and humerus), Harris Lines form when a dietary insult has occurred. Something interrupts the growth of the bone, and then it begins to grow again. The opacity in the bone—seen most often in the tibia or femur and represented as thin white lines which run perpendicularly across the long-bone shaft—indicates that the insult to the bone had passed. Many people have such lines, which may reflect a poor diet or a dietary absorption problem. These lines are also known to remodel out as one grows older.

The strongest evidence regarding the physical profile of the child was skeletal because, other than her face, she had very little soft tissue preserved. This most likely was a result of how long she had been in the coffin and the liquid material in the coffin. Generally speaking, she had been a healthy child skeletally, and no perimortem injuries were visible.

Chemistry samples from several regions across the face were analyzed by Dr. Frank Fronzcek, who had helped us on more than one occasion with the analysis of historic coffin remains. He determined that more than likely the material on her face was mold that had grown rapidly once the body was exposed to fresh air. Dr. Karen Ross, the pathologist, also had taken samples from the little tissue that was preserved (facial region, abdomen, pelvis, legs, skull). All results were inconclusive due to deterioration of the tissue.

In terms of clothing, the child wore a cotton dimity dress with a checkered pattern covering a chemise and pantalets. The only personal artifacts found in the coffin included two religious medals and a cross around her neck. One of the medals was of the Virgin Mary holding the Christ child. The other had a female with the inscription "Saint Philomina Pray for Us." The wearing of such medals is associated with Roman Catholicism. Saint Philomina is the patron saint of youth (often spelled "Philomena" in modern times).

At the end of the initial evaluation process that day, we opened the envelope provided by the Toups family. The child the family thought might possibly be the one in the coffin was Berthe (or Bertha) Lambert. Berthe died August 23, 1874, and was buried on August 30, 1877. She was just three years of age when she died.

We presented multiple facts to the Toups descendants that pointed to Berthe's not being the child in the coffin. The child

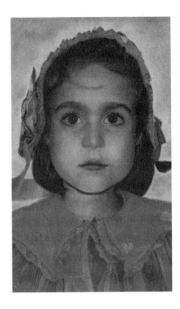

Figure 27. 2-D facial reconstruction of child from historic coffin; image enhanced.

from the coffin appeared to be somewhat older than Berthe's age of three years—again, more than likely five to five and one-half years old. This assessment was based on the dental development and the long-bone growth. Evaluation of the clothing also pointed to an era earlier than the 1870s. Some of it was identical in style and manufacturer to clothing the textile expert had analyzed from an earlier, mid-nineteenth-century burial. The cast iron coffin clearly was a ringer for the 1848 design by Fisk. Could it have been archived in some store from 1853 until 1877, a quarter of a century later, having survived the Civil War and upheaval in the South following the war? Of course anything is possible, but we just did not believe this added up.

Our summation of the child's profile noted that she was five to five and one-half years of age and that most likely she was buried in the mid-nineteenth century, possibly the 1850s.

Earlier, we had suggested to the Toups family that we could complete a facial reconstruction on the child to represent what she may have looked like in life if they wished for us to do so. They did. Since the skull was so fragile, we decided to do a two-dimensional image rather than subject the fragile bone to a clay image. The process included taking photographs of the child's skull, adding facial-tissue depth markers for a child of that age, and then completing a line drawing of the face. The line drawing would then be enhanced in Photoshop. Figure 27 is the image Eileen Barrow completed for the child.

Approximately a year after the initial analysis on the child's remains, a graduate student in human ecology at LSU was conducting archival work on the clothing from this case and found a name that might well be the name of the child in the coffin. A birth-baptismal record recorded with the Diocese of Houma-Thibodaux reflects that Ema Toups, daughter of Pierre Toups and Ophelia Pontiff, was baptized at St. Joseph's Catholic Cathedral in Thibodaux on December 13, 1846. A subsequent funeral record, from the same diocese's archives office, reflects that Ema Toups died on April 27, 1852. At the time, she was approximately five and one-half years of age. Both the family and FACES Lab scientists believe the child from the coffin is Ema Toups.

In a case like this, what happens to the remains and artifacts? The decision rests with the family. The Toups descendants placed Ema in the single vault with the rest of her family, donated the coffin (which was bound for destruction) to the LSU Rural Life Museum, and donated the clothing to the LSU Human Ecology Textile and Clothing Museum. All other artifacts went to the family.

Some persons might ask, Why remove the child from the coffin and analyze the remains? Why not just leave her at rest? Perpetual care for such vault burials requires a considerable investment of funding on the part of the family and the diocese. Multiple tombs make costs that much greater. Many Catholic cemeteries have simply run out of space for new plots. In order to continue to bury individual family members in the same cemetery close to their loved ones, the tradition over the years has been to remove coffins and caskets and other large artifacts from the vaults after a certain number of years of interment if additional bodies need to be added to a tomb. This practice makes space for subsequent family members who die to be placed within the vault.

The discovery of Ema's unidentified coffin allowed the FACES Lab an opportunity to participate in solving a historical mystery, one which the Toups family wished to be solved. It also allowed us to add knowledge to the scientific record regarding the preservation of human remains and to the historical record for that place and period. We are indebted to the Toups family and particularly to Ms. Merlin Simek for her generosity and desire to seek the truth about the child in the tomb.

10. Cat's Paw

U nusual cases seem to gravitate toward the FACES Lab. We have dealt with paper-mache skulls, alien-like guitar fish, a fake "bigfoot" print, an ostrich humerus with a prosthesis, and wild and domestic animals galore. Yet there always seems to be room for a new first. Such was the case we received from north Louisiana.

One day we were presented with what clearly was the forelimb of a sizable animal: the humerus, the radius, the ulna, and the forepaw. It was large, very large. Nothing else from the animal had been found in the north Louisiana woods where this limited portion of the body had been discovered. We x-rayed it, and then we removed the tissue. The distal phalanges had been cut off at some point in the past, suggesting a declawing of something big, bad, and probably ugly. We just did not know what. It was time to call in our resident LSU Vet School go-to man, Dr. Ray Wilhite. Though Ray is no longer at the LSU Vet School in Baton Rouge, we certainly were glad that he was here at that time.

Ray took one look at it and said to me, "Mary, you have some kind of cat here, a very large cat. . . . I'm just not sure what kind of cat it is." I asked him to explain how he knew immediately that it was a cat, and he pointed to a little opening, called a foramen on the medial portion of the distal humerus (figure 28). That, he said, is called a supracondylar foramen. Every cat has one, even small, domesticated cats.

We all then began to speculate about what kind of cat could possibly have a forelimb so large and muscular, had its claws removed, and ended up in the woods in north Louisiana. Ray took the bones to the LSU Vet School to get some assistance in sorting out the mystery. He called a few days later with the news. He told us we had an African lion's forelimb. That information only added

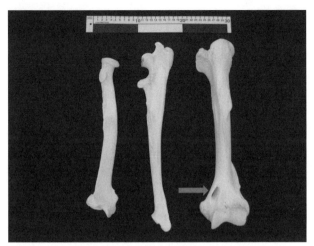

Figure 28. Forelimb of African lion found in north Louisiana woods.

to the mystery. A subsequent call to the Bossier Parish Sheriff's Office helped to confirm the vet school's identification. It seems the sheriff's office had finally located a man who lived in the area who said that his family had owned an African lion for years, that it had died of natural causes, and that they had buried it in the woods. Interestingly, none of the rest of the animal was ever found.

The sheriff's office donated the forelimb to the FACES Lab to use in classes, especially in our outreach program where we visit local schools and talk with students about forensic anthropology. High-school students seem the most curious about it, while primary-school students seem to take in stride the fact that the lion was in the woods. What's so unusual about an African lion in the north Louisiana woods? Beats me! Only in Louisiana.

11. In a Cotton Field

In the summer of 2010, a farmer was plowing his cotton field in Natchitoches Parish in northwestern Louisiana when he hit something with his plow near the edge of the road. He got off his tractor to see what it was and discovered a human skull. He called the sheriff. Sheriff's deputies and the coroner, Dr. Curtis, arrived at the scene and soon noticed that more than just a skull was present. The coroner called me.

When we arrived at the site after a three-hour drive, the sheriff's deputies and coroner's investigators were there waiting for us. They had placed a canopy over the remains to help shade us from the sun. A recreational vehicle was parked nearby for our needs, and food and drink were plentiful.

Natchitoches Parish soil is full of iron oxide and has an orange tint to it. As we began the slow process of excavating the bones, we could tell that the dried-out bones had taken on the color of the soil. They, too, had an orange tint. Since bone is porous and will take on the color of the soil around it after a considerable period of time, we believed we were working with remains that had been there for quite some time. We noticed all of the old home sites around the area and speculated the farmer may have happened upon an old grave site. But was the "burial" formal or clandestine, one that someone had tried to hide? Our imaginations began to take off. Deliberate burial? Saturday-night fight where someone was killed and simply hidden away in a cotton field? Someone who had been hit by a car accidentally quite a few years before and no one had seen anything? We had no idea at the time just how far from the truth we really were.

Enter the regional archaeologist, Dr. Jeff Gerrard. Jeff came along a few hours after we had set up our archaeological burial unit, while we were recovering the remains. One of the things we were intrigued about was the fact that the remains were very shallow, just below the farmer's plow zone. They clearly were not buried the usual three feet or so down. (Almost no one is ever buried six feet under.)

Also, as best as we could tell, no obvious clothing was present on the bones. The bones had no odor, were completely clean, and were all dried out. Jeff had an idea. He asked what I thought of the possibility that the remains could be those of a soldier. "A soldier? And what war might that be," I asked.

"Why, the Civil War," he said. I rested back on my heels and contemplated that suggestion for a very long moment. Though I could not see the coroner's representative at the time, I felt that if she had heard that suggestion she might be breathing a sigh of relief.

Jeff went on to explain that the location where we were working was just down the river from what had been a fairly significant local battle of the Civil War, one that was called the Battle of Minotte's Ferry. Though I had worked on several Civil War sites over the years, Minotte's Ferry was not one with which I was familiar. We kept digging. I knew that whatever we pulled out of the ground would first have to go back to the FACES Laboratory and be analyzed before we could even begin to decide whether it might be a soldier who was covered over by a few inches of dirt some 150 years earlier.

As we continued digging, I thought about the archaeological work we had conducted over the years at multiple Civil War sites and the metal buttons we often had found representing both Union and Confederate armies. I wondered if we would be fortunate enough to find such metal buttons, if indeed this was a soldier.

In the field, instead of metal buttons, we found a few, small, white buttons in the soil, but no clothing remnants. Also, in the area of the feet, we found metal fragments. Additionally, we found some type of metal material near the waist.

We loaded everything into our vehicle and began the long trek home. Jeff's suggestion was an intriguing possibility. We could not wait to get back to Baton Rouge to do preliminary x-rays of the body. Was it a nineteenth-century case or a twentieth-century case?

Back at the lab, our measurements of the skull and our observations of non-metric traits on the skull (those characteristics that can suggest ancestry but are not measurable) indicated that the skeletal remains were those of a white individual: narrow nasal opening, sloping eye orbits, straight face, towering nasal bones, among others. The skull also told us that it was a male. The sloping forehead, large brow ridge, large muscle-attachment sites, blunt superior eye orbit margins, large mastoid process, square chin, and 90-degree gonial angle on the mandible, all supported maleness. Though the skull's features and measurements told us what we needed to know, we always defer to the hip bone (innominate) to assign sex if we have a hip bone. The hip bone had a narrow sciatic notch and multiple other characteristics that confirmed male as the proper assignment. The hip bone also told us what we needed to know about age; the auricular surface, which is the region on each hip bone that articulates with the sacrum, was youthful in appearance and had not begun to take on the signs of major aging. The faces of the pubic bones, referred to as the pubic symphyses, also appeared quite young with evidence of billowing and youthful ridges still present. We assigned the young white male an age somewhere between twenty and twenty-five.

As we began to analyze the x-rays we had made, we realized that the young man had multiple lead fragments lodged in his skeleton and at least one fairly obvious perimortem injury to one of his ribs. The lead fragments were bullets.

Next, we began to discover additional buttons, small white porcelain buttons, the same kind I had seen over and over again in the Civil War soldier burials I had worked on some twenty years earlier at Port Hudson, a battleground in East Feliciana Parish, Louisiana. As we began to clean the piece of metal found near the waist, we discovered it was part a buckle, identical to others we had seen at Port Hudson. Finally, metal from the area where the young man's shoes would have been present turned out to be shanks from boots.

Several of the multiple lead bullets provided additional information. Though deformed when entering the bone, they more than likely came from the Civil War era. It seemed we did have a Civil War soldier's remains and not those of anyone from the recent past. Our report to the parish coroner noted that conclusion, and contact with the regional archaeologist and state archaeologist culminated with a decision to rebury the soldier on hallowed ground.

Speaking of hallowed ground, there once was a project that never really got off the ground but that involved authenticating supposed grave sites to be those of Civil War soldiers, in particular Confederate soldiers. Someone thought I was going to be "disturbing Civil War soldiers who were at rest" and notified me by email that he "would be standing on the ridge with his rifle." I rarely feel afraid or threatened in my job, but this man got my attention. He also got the attention of the FBI, who paid him a visit and convinced him that it was a good idea to never have contact with me again. Every once in a while I think about that veiled threat, wondering what would have happened if our project had gone as scheduled. I, of course, would have been there, as usual, helping to recover the past, though with a cautious look over my shoulder on occasion.

12. The USS *Monitor* and Her Crew

On December 30, 1862, the USS *Monitor*, an ironclad warship, was being guided to shore in turbulent seas off the coast of Cape Hatteras, North Carolina, when it sank beneath the waves, ending up on the ocean's floor. Sixteen of the fifty-nine seamen on board were lost—and never found.

Commissioned in February 1862, *Monitor* gained notoriety for its Civil War battle with the ironclad CSS *Virginia*, which the South had refurbished from the USS *Merrimack.* The battle of ironclads began on March 9, 1862, at Hampton Roads, Virginia, and lasted for several days, with the *Virginia* being somewhat bested by *Monitor.* However, less than a year later, Mother Nature handed *Monitor* that devastating fate.

On a summer day in 2007, I met Dr. Wayne Smith, an archaeologist from Texas A&M University and a member of a special commission created in association with the USS *Monitor* project. Wayne just happened to be in Baton Rouge to consult with Dr. Heather McKillop, one of my colleagues, about conservation of wooden artifacts she had recovered in her archaeology work in Belize. That introduction at the LSU FACES Laboratory led to a collaborative research project several years later between the lab, Smith, and the U.S. Mariner Museum in Washington, D.C.

Monitor sits at a depth of 240 feet below the Atlantic Ocean's surface, sixteen miles offshore from Cape Hatteras, North Carolina. When it sank, its most iconic feature, the armored gun turret, was displaced, ending up beneath the ship's hull. The exact location of the *Monitor* has been known since 1973. However, it was not until the late 1990s that part of it was raised, the propeller and shaft. In 2002, the gun turret was brought to the surface.

Once the turret was raised, archaeologists began the daunting task of literally excavating the materials inside of it. That task was made more difficult because a thick layer of debris had turned to sludge; that sludge was made even denser by rotting organic matter from the sea. The archaeologists' progress was slow, but in the process of excavation, they recovered a boot, multiple pieces of silverware, a gold ring, a comb, a knife, a few other personal possessions, and, surprisingly, two fairly complete sets of human skeletal remains. More than likely, the cold water and debris in the turret had helped to preserve the remains and kept them from floating away from the ship. Scientists had no idea who the men might be out of the sixteen seamen who lost their lives.

Following recovery, the bones were shipped to JPAC in Hawaii—the Joint Prisoners of War, Missing in Action Accounting Command—for analysis by their forensic anthropologists. The JPAC anthropologists are charged with accounting for Americans lost in past conflicts. Their team concluded that both of the males were white (at least one and perhaps more black seamen had been on *Monitor* when it sank). The anthropologists also determined that one of the sailors was between seventeen and twenty-four years of age, and the other was somewhere between thirty and forty.

A plan began to create a documentary about *Monitor* and these two young men. Part of the plan would include facial reconstructions of what the two unknown seamen may have looked like in life. Our FACES Lab had the expertise to develop the facsimiles and a long record of helping indentify unknown persons, sometimes decades after death. I knew immediately that I wanted our lab to assist if possible.

Leaders in the *Monitor* project embraced our willingness to perform free of charge the service of recreating faces of the two men, and they made arrangements to have replicas of the skulls sent to us. Within a matter of weeks following our agreement to work on the project, a large black suitcase containing the replicas of the skull and hip bones for each of the men arrived at our lab. Upon close examination of the replicas, I concluded that I agreed with the designations of age and ancestry provided by JPAC. The older of the two individuals had grooves in his teeth where the enamel had worn down. This suggested to JPAC and to us that he might have smoked a pipe.

For the next two years, Wayne and I went back and forth with the project managers, who were trying to secure a national venue for filming and promoting the project. Out of the blue, one day in early January 2012, Wayne called, and he and I agreed that a summer completion date for the project was reasonable for our lab and that we could begin the reconstructions. Within a few days, I received phone calls from him and other persons connected to the project asking if we could finish the reconstructions and have them in Washington by March 6. A ceremony was to take place that day marking the 150th anniversary of the Battle of Hampton Roads. Organizers hoped to have facial images of the two men for the ceremony. Though we knew it would be difficult to do, we agreed to try to have the images ready by that time.

As part of the project, LSU's University Relations Department graciously agreed to take photographs of our step-by-step process of creating three-dimensional clay facial reconstructions of the seamen. We also planned to enhance those images once they were finished, using a software program to make them appear more lifelike.

Eileen Barrow began the tedious process of completing the facial images. First, she cut tissue-depth markers to very specific lengths for approximately thirty-two areas across the face. The tissue-depth markers are just very small cylindrical erasers cut to various lengths to match the average soft-tissue depths at certain landmarks across the face. For example, the area just above the eyes in the middle of the forehead has soft tissue that typically is approximately four to five millimeters thick, while the soft tissue in the cheek area is very thick, ranging from fourteen or so millimeters to more than twenty. These depths have been documented by our laboratory (and others using various techniques) through a research project using ultrasound technology to scan close to one thousand persons of known age, sex, and ancestry to come up with tissue-depth averages for different locations across the face. Once all of the markers are glued in place, clay is then added to create the appearance of tissue.

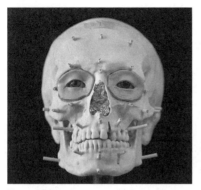

Figure 29. *Monitor* seaman's skull replica with facial-tissue depth markers.

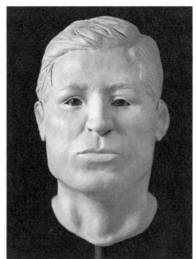

Figure 30. Completed 3-D clay facial reconstruction of older *Monitor* seaman.

Some forensic sculptors add simulated muscles before placing the final finishing clay on the face's surface; others do not.

Additionally, we have formulae to recreate the nose based on the boney structure of the nose, the width of the nasal opening, and other attributes. In recreating the lips, generally speaking, one uses the distance from gumline to gumline for height of the lips, and from canine tooth to canine tooth for the width of the mouth. Prosthetic eyes are set into the skull in very specific ways that take into account the shape of the eye orbit.

Forensic sculptors who have been doing facial reconstructions for years often have formulated their own personal protocol for creating a three-dimensional image that might not always adhere to a standard technique. Therefore, certain aspects of such forensic imaging include more subjective preferences for a specific way of building the face.

Figure 29 is the basic skull with partial clay attachment for the thirty-year-old man. Figure 30 is the clay rendering of what he may

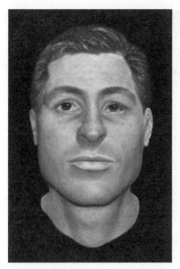

Figure 31. Computer-enhanced image of older *Monitor* seaman.

Figure 32. Computer-enhanced image of older *Monitor* seaman with beard.

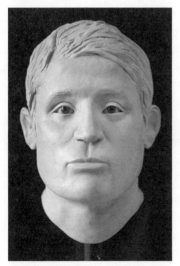

Figure 33. Completed 3-D clay facial reconstruction of younger *Monitor* seaman.

Figure 34. Computer-enhanced image of younger *Monitor* seaman.

Figure 35. Scanning of younger *Monitor* seaman's 3-D clay reconstruction prior to printing in ABS plastic.

have looked like in life. Once the clay facial reconstruction was complete, Eileen took photographs of the image and used Photoshop to give the young man more lifelike qualities. Figure 31 is the image of what the thirty-year-old seaman looked like after computer enhancement. Figure 32 is the same image with a beard. For the younger of the two men, we did much of the same. Figure 33 is the finished image from clay, and figure 34 is the computer-enhanced image. We did not provide a beard for him after having examined quite a few historic photos that suggested a man his age might have been clean shaven, though we have no way of knowing that. Also, figure 35 illustrates the process by which the clay images were scanned and ultimately "printed" as three-dimensional sculptures in a common thermoplastic known as ABS (acrylonitrile butadiene styrene). These ABS plastic models are held in our archives.

On March 6, 2012, research associate Nicole Harris, who had assisted with much of the transportation logistics and computer scanning, and I traveled to Washington to the official unveiling of the images created by our lab. The clay reconstructions had been transported to Virginia via air by UPS, their donation to the project.

One of the major reasons for creating facial reconstructions of the young men was because their identity is unknown. It is the hope of the Mariner Museum staff that one or both of the images may look familiar to someone, especially if their family history suggests a relative was on board the ironclad that fateful day. DNA comparisons to potential family members might give one or both of these young men a name. No one knows who was in the gun turret that day at that specific time, though a manifest listed persons on board the ship. Genealogists continue to work toward providing the two men with names.

On March 8, 2013, the two *Monitor* sailors were laid to rest at Arlington National Cemetery. Researchers have no plans to raise the ship itself. Whether other sets of human skeletal remains are present in its hull may never be known. However, the vessel already has the distinction of being a formal cemetery and a final resting place of the dead, protected by federal law.

13. Victims of the Ku Klux Klan

One day in 2008, Dr. Janet McDonald of Syracuse University called me with an interesting proposition. McDonald told me that she was a law professor at Syracuse in New York and was wondering if I would be interested in helping her with a cause that was close to her heart. Her project is called the Syracuse University College of Law Cold Case Justice Initiative. She and some of her students are reviewing several cases from the 1960s where young black men may have been murdered by the Ku Klux Klan. Now, in the 1960s in Louisiana, if someone was a member of the Klan, that person usually did not talk about it. However, some fifty years later, times have changed. McDonald and Mr. Stanley Nelson, editor of the *Concordia Sentinel,* had joined forces to work on cases from east-central Louisiana. Stanley has had a vested interest in many cases from the Concordia Parish area for years and has written close to two hundred newspaper articles on those cases.

One case was that of Mr. Frank Morris, a part-time radio gospel host and successful businessman. Morris owned a shoe repair shop that employed several people. His store was set on fire with him in it on December 10, 1964. From his hospital bed, he told investigators that he was asleep in his store around 2:00 a.m. when he heard the sound of breaking glass, according to a newspaper article written by Nelson. Morris was forced back into the store when he tried to leave, and the subsequent gasoline explosion set him on fire. He ran from the back of the store in flames. He lived for four painful days and finally succumbed to his injuries. Before his death, Morris was interviewed by the FBI and told agents that he thought he recognized the men who committed the crime and that he had considered them friends at the time.

Nelson has written extensively on the Morris case and has investigated every lead he could find. He is determined to solve this case, and the Morris family believes in Stanley Nelson. So do I.

Another case in which both Nelson and McDonald are interested is that of Joseph Edwards. There are those who believe that the same people who set Morris's store on fire may have been involved with Edwards's case. Just a teenager when he went missing in Concordia Parish, Edwards would drive his car up and down the highway, feeling really good about himself and the world in general. He was an employee at the Shamrock Motel in Vidalia, Louisiana, when on the night of July 11, 1964, he disappeared. He was last seen around 11:00 p.m. at the motel, and witnesses have said that he was seen being pulled over by law enforcement that night on the Ferriday-Vidalia Highway. His car was found abandoned later. What happened to Edwards? Many believe he was a victim of the Ku Klux Klan. Their involvement in his disappearance has never been proven. Where did he go? During the 1950s, the eastern part of Louisiana was somewhat of a hotbed of the Klan. The Klan had operated in that area for more than seventy-five years and was a force with which to be reckoned. Some say that the situation had not really changed in the 1960s.

One of the reasons that McDonald had contacted the FACES Lab was that she had heard that on at least one occasion we had recovered some human skeletal remains from up in that region. McDonald was referring to a skull cap, the calotte, that a man's dog had dragged up one day in Clayton, Louisiana, in 2002. At the time I received the phone call from the local sheriff, I had gathered several graduate students and made the trip to Clayton. We surveyed multiple acres that day across the road from a row of houses, trying to see if we could find anything else that might indicate that a person's remains were nearby. The calotte was definitely human but was not complete enough to tell us much other than that it most likely was a male, under the age of fifty or so. It was all dried out and had been exposed to the elements for quite some time. After searching for hours, we called it quits and went home.

In 2009, as part of our new database for unidentified and missing people, we had the calotte tested for DNA. Nuclear DNA from a small section of the calotte provided only an incomplete profile. At that point, we decided to send samples to Dr. Artie Eisner at the DNA laboratory at North Texas University to perform mitochondrial DNA analysis. Artie's lab is one of only a handful in the entire country capable of carrying out Mito profiling because of the expense of setting up such a lab and the expertise required to run it. Ultimately, Artie's lab provided us with a profile for the calotte.

Mrs. Julia Dobbins of Bridge City, Louisiana, Joseph Edwards's sister, provided a DNA sample to determine if the skull cap was a DNA family match. The mitochondrial DNA results reflected that the skull cap we had found did not belong to a relative of Joseph Edwards. In fact, in 2011 someone stepped forward and said that the skull cap actually may have come from a cemetery that was not too far from the neighborhood where it was found. One of the first questions we had asked when we originally worked this case was whether a cemetery was in the immediate area. The reason for that question is that sometimes old graves erode and animals find remains. Though we were not made aware of the proximity of the cemetery to the discovery site at the time, the skull cap may indeed be from the old cemetery.

Disappointing to say the least with regard to the skull cap, Joseph Edwards remains missing. Both McDonald and Nelson hope to some day have additional information that can lead them and us to finding and identifying Edwards. In recent years, the FBI has begun to reevaluate more than one hundred cold cases from the Ku Klux Klan days. Joseph Edwards's case is one of those. Perhaps some day we will help put him to rest.

14. Hurricane Isaac

August 29, 2012. They called it a "slow-moving" storm, and they said it was "big." Packing winds of less than one hundred miles per hour and crawling along like a baby just learning how to slide across the floor, Hurricane Isaac approached southern Louisiana. Seven years to the day almost after Katrina destroyed much of New Orleans and surrounding areas. Unlike Katrina, where authorities called for evacuation and many stayed, people left town on the run when the weathermen said Isaac was heading straight for New Orleans and Baton Rouge. Though those two cities would see fallen trees, power loss, and moderate flooding damage, things were different in St. John and Plaquemines parishes, and surrounding parishes.

Forecasters certainly were correct about the speed of the storm. Isaac rolled into Louisiana and simply sat down, not moving, building and building a storm surge, pouring and pouring rain over some of the southern parishes. By the time it was over, it had ushered in a fourteen-foot storm surge that undermined levees and destroyed or severely damaged almost sixty thousand homes. Loss of community was devastating. Part of that sense of lost community was the disruption of Promised Land, English Turn, and Bertrandville cemeteries on the east bank of the Mississippi River in Plaquemines Parish.

After the storm, authorities witnessed an eerie sight when they approached those cemeteries, two of which had existed since the 1800s and are still in use today as final resting places for loved ones in the local community. Highway 39, which follows the river, was blocked not only by houses that had floated from their foundations but also by concrete vaults, tombs, and caskets that had been lifted from their moorings and tossed along the highway. Some of the tombs were still intact while others were broken open with waterlogged caskets resting inside. Still other caskets were gone completely and scattered human remains dotted the road and the grass between the vaults.

An email late one afternoon from Henri Yenni, with Louisiana's Department of Health and Hospitals (DHH), came as no surprise. For years, many of us in Louisiana who deal with the dead had been trying to jump-start a state disaster team that could handle smaller disasters, certainly not one the size of Katrina, but any that might result in minimum impact in terms of lost lives or cemetery disruption. Henri and I discussed the possibility of assistance from the FACES Laboratory with the damage created by Isaac, and he put me in touch with Arbie Goings. Arbie and I had worked together on various cemetery recovery projects through the national disaster teams. DHH had hired him to manage the damage done by Isaac in Plaquemines cemeteries.

Discussions with Arbie led to a roundtable meeting with my research associates in the laboratory. We outlined the pros and cons of such assistance as we might give to DHH and finally concluded that the recovery and identification process were manageable. I knew all of the team had to be on board or the logistics might be difficult. The fall semester at LSU had begun, and two of us had teaching obligations.

We decided to rotate various team members in and out of the work cycle and take graduate students with us as needed to round out the team. For both the seasoned graduate students and those new ones who had just entered our program (eleven in all), they would receive the experience of a lifetime. Requirements for participation in the burial identification process included written evidence that all of the new students had their series of shots that are required by the lab to touch human remains. These included Hepatitis A and B and tetanus. Those who had simply started their series of shots would only be allowed to act as scribes. All wanted to go, and all wanted to take part. Their participation proved essential to the successful completion of the effort.

We began to organize the tools we would need to carry with us. They included our typical portable backpacks that we usually take into wooded areas, but they also included our measurement tools such as calipers and collapsible osteometric boards. We had been informed that air-conditioned tents with floors would be waiting for us upon arrival. In the tents would be large tables made of sawhorses and sheets of plywood.

Much of our gear included personal protection. We would be covered from head to toe and would change the gear for each case. The soiled gear then would be collected by Plaquemines Parish workers and transported to hazardous waste sites.

We quickly gathered forms to use in recording information about each individual. Those forms went into packets for each burial and included those we typically use in forensic cases as well as others adapted from various sources. There were skeletal inventory forms, dental charts, clothing forms, casket description forms, pathology forms, and several others. Also, each set of human remains would receive a unique number assigned only to that person. We requested that Arbie number all damaged vaults both inside and outside the cemeteries. He had already begun to do so and included GPS coordinates for each displaced tomb or vault. Some skeletal remains had been transported to a more secure area early on in the recovery process and would need to be re-incorporated into the cemetery population. They consisted of human remains that had been strewn throughout Isaac's path and were lying out in the open after the storm. They, too, were given numbers specific only to them. The GPS coordinates would prove useful later on in re-associating individuals.

For almost three weeks, on various days, we made the two-hour drive to the west bank of the Mississippi River and then picked up the ferry for transport back to the east bank. Arbie and I had decided that we would begin our work at Promised Land cemetery. As we drove down Highway 39 along the eastern edge of the Mississippi River levee, we saw the many homes that had been ravaged by the storm surge. The water marks on the houses suggested that at least four or five feet of water had sat inside the houses, perhaps for several days. Furniture was out by the road; doors were off their

Figure 36. Vaults and tombs displaced along Highway 39 by Hurricane Isaac.

hinges; many houses had already been gutted in anticipation of rebuilding.

On the faces of the few residents and their friends and family who were there to assist them, we saw grim evidence of Mother Nature's havoc. With slow, deliberate movement, they continued to pick through what was left of a lifetime of memories. They hardly raised their heads as we passed by. I often looked away, not wanting to intrude on their tragedy. Later on, I would remember the looks on their faces that day and on the days to come. When one of them walked close to where we were working one day, he sadly stated to anyone within earshot, "I wish that half the attention that is being paid to the dead would be paid to the living." I have not forgotten the weariness of that man's face, the frustration in his voice, the slump of his shoulders as he walked on.

In the first few days of our work, debris was still piled almost to the top of the levee.

Someone pointed out that, if the storm surge had been much greater, much of the debris, including quite a few tombs, would have topped the levee and gone right on down the Mississippi River.

As we neared Promised Land, tombs began to dot the highway, both sides of the highway. One vault was more than 1.2 miles from Promised Land. When we finally got to Promised Land after weaving in and out among large trucks trying to pick up the debris, we saw that just beyond the cemetery a large house sat halfway across the road, impeding the flow of traffic.

We got out of our vehicles and took in the cemetery for the first time. Blue tarps were everywhere. Tombs rested on top of other tombs. Some were broken open with nothing inside other than a small piece of a casket, attesting to the fact that a body had once rested there. Name plates were missing from the tombs. Some tombs were even crushed by other tombs. Caskets were out of their tombs, and old caskets, especially, were broken open, revealing their contents. One tomb had floated to the house nearest the cemetery and was wedged into the kitchen window. Another tomb sat on the house's back patio.

When we first viewed the destruction, the task seemed daunting. I wondered what I had gotten us into, how we could handle the massive destruction, and how we could bring order to the chaos. Then, I realized it was something we did on a routine basis—simply one case at a time.

A daily round-trip to the east bank of Plaquemines Parish could last a minimum of five hours in travel time alone, according to how busy the ferry was that day and how heavy the traffic. When we first began the work, very few private citizens seemed to be riding the ferry. Most were in utility vehicles, National Guard personnel, FEMA, parish, and other local authorities. Highway 39 had law enforcement vehicles all over the place at the ferry landing, understandable since the area was still without power. A night-time curfew was also still in effect.

Arbie had set up two collection areas, one at English Turn Cemetery and one at Promised Land. At Promised Land many caskets had already been rounded up and placed under blue tarps, rows and rows of caskets.

Also, throughout the cemetery, blue tarps (all too familiar

Figure 37. Tarp-covered caskets displaced by Hurricane Isaac.

from Katrina days) were thrown across damaged vaults. We slowly counted them—five here, six or seven there. We estimated that, on that day, we had approximately twenty or more sets of remains that needed our attention at the cemetery. We set to work.

We had established two workstations inside the tent and began to analyze two burials at a time. Each team had multiple anthropologists and a scribe whose job was strictly to take notes and fill in the information needed to try to identify the body. Our job was simple: We would open each casket, photograph the contents, describe everything we could see; then profile the individual within the casket—black male, black female, young vs. elderly, short versus tall, and so forth.

At the end of each day, all forms were brought back to our lab at LSU. We would look over the forms, sign off on them, and then scan them in order for the scanned sheets of information to be placed on a thumb drive for Arbie to try and sort through to see if those without names could be matched to descriptions of those missing.

In some cases, personal items within the caskets helped to

identify the person inside: memorial cards with the obituary on it, a hospital tag with name and date, perhaps a prosthetic device for a hip replacement. Family members came and went as we worked, providing personal information about their loved ones: clothing they were wearing, the color and type of casket in which they were buried. Many of those buried in the cemeteries were elderly individuals, their dates of death ranging from the 1970s to 2012.

One man described how his wife's casket was no longer where it was supposed to be. He told the story of his family, how long he had been married, and how important it was to place his wife back where she belonged. She had been dead for many years. I do not know if she was found.

The weight of the caskets was a deterrent to our success. It took five or six large men to pick up a heavy casket and get it to the tent. In the first few days of the process, we had the assistance of a group of young men from Oregon who had been there for almost a week. They were businessmen who had traveled to Louisiana to volunteer their assistance in helping clean out houses and offered to help with the cemetery recovery work. They belong to an organization known as "Rubicon" and travel across the country to assist in mass disasters. On the way home that first day after meeting them, we talked about the name of their organization and remembered that in school at one point we had heard about "crossing the Rubicon." We googled it and found out that it was related to the name of a river that was important in a battle involving Julius Caesar, though its exact location has been lost to history. It referred to the fact that once one crossed the Rubicon, there was no going back. That phrase is one we surely will use in the future for some of our work.

The Rubicon volunteers were not the only ones who helped us, but were among the more memorable. We also had assistance from a church group from Texas that had moved into New Orleans as a very large group and had fanned out all over southern Louisiana to help in the disaster effort.

Part of the recovery process involved familiarizing ourselves with terminology used by funeral-home directors in discussing burials.

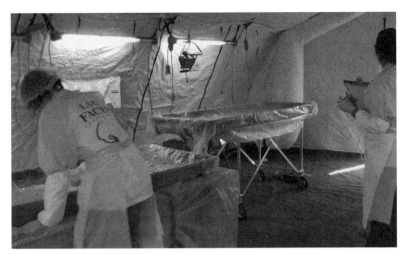

Figure 38. Portable morgue in Plaquemines Parish set up for Hurricane Isaac.

First, there is the "casket." During the late 1800s, metal caskets began to be produced on a large scale and started to gain popularity over what in the past had been a store-bought or homemade wooden "coffin." Many still refer to wooden burial containers today as coffins. Others call them wooden caskets. Then comes the "vault" into which the casket or coffin may be placed. Vaults are made to hold caskets and offer them some measure of protection. Some vaults are sealed; others are not. Vaults normally are made for one casket; however, some can accommodate two caskets, one on top of the other. Usually, they are made of concrete, either lined or unlined. Sometimes, they are made of polymer or metal. Also, vaults may not have a bottom in them. Vaults are either buried completely underground or may be buried partially with a portion of the vault above the ground. Unfortunately, these vaults can float like small boats if buoyed by enough wind and water. ("Crypt" and "vault" can be used interchangeably.)

Crypts are a little different. The term "crypt" refers to the actual space or area that accommodates a casket in a tomb or mausoleum.

A "tomb" is a structure with one or more crypts (usually four). It is the tomb where "re-use" occurs, especially in south Louisiana.

"Re-use" refers to inserting multiple family members within the tomb over time. Tombs are made of brick, concrete, cinder block, marble, granite, or a combination of these materials. These tombs may also be moved by water.

Finally, a "mausoleum" is a single structure with multiple crypts. Some mausoleum crypts hold one casket, and some can accommodate two. Mausoleums are usually very well made and will not float away during a flood. Mausoleums also can be quite large. New Orleans is famous for its multiple tombs which can rise to the level of mausoleum if their creators so desire and if the building is large enough to accommodate many family members. Some mausoleums are made for one specific person, especially if that individual is famous and rich enough to afford the lavish burial display.

Then, we had to consider the caskets or coffins themselves. John Vickers and Gary Tranchina were there the first few days of the recovery project. They both have been associated with funeral homes for years and knew exactly what the names of many caskets were and other details that would prove helpful in documenting them. If they were not sure about an older casket, Gary would access the online catalogues that had both descriptions and photographs of the casket style.

The recovery effort would not have been possible, nor would our efforts have been as successful, if we had not had the assistance of Mike Mudge with the Plaquemines Parish Sheriff's Office. Mike had led the effort to restore much of Plaquemines Parish after Katrina devastated it but had experienced a heart attack in the years following Katrina. However, that did not slow him down at all, and he was there every day helping with the recovery effort at the cemeteries and helping with anything we needed from the parish. He is an unsung hero in all of this.

Family members also were helpful because they remembered what kind of casket and what color the casket was if the burial had taken place in recent years. Casket manufacturers, such as Batesville, Newpointe, and York became names we heard over and over again. We would hear "fixed handle" versus "swing handle."

We would learn to call the decorative metal on the side handles "lugs" and those on the ends of the caskets "corner covers." We would learn if a casket was made of 16-, 18-, or 20-gauge metal, with 16-gauge representing a thicker metal.

"Full couch" or "half couch" were terms which described the actual top cover of a casket. In the full couch model, the entire top of the casket opened as a single unit. Half couch referred to whether the top cover was divided into two separate parts with hinges for both.

One of the more important pieces of information we learned was that some of the caskets had a small, glass tube on the end. The tube, typically about three inches long, is known as a "memorial tube" and should contain a paper scroll. Written on that scroll should be the deceased individual's name, date of death, and sometimes other information, such as the funeral home that buried him or her. We would come to look for those tubes with great anticipation because we knew that, if they were present, the identity of that particular body might be swift. We were soon disappointed to find that many of the caskets did not have the memorial tubes, and some that did had empty tubes. Those that did have something inside would set up a round of hushed breathing while a member of our team slowly opened the metal screw cap and carefully pulled the fragile scroll from the glass tube with a pair of tweezers. Disappointment was great when the scroll was blank. Either it had never been filled out or had been filled out with ink. Number two pencils should always be used in entomology containers and in memorial tubes.

In traditional forensic cases, when we recover entomological evidence, we put a small piece of paper in the alcohol-filled vial with the evidence. On that paper, we write with a number two pencil exactly where the evidence came from, the date, and so forth. Number two pencils are also supposed to be used in the memorial tubes in a casket as well. If ink is used, either written with a pen or from a computer printer, the ink will lift away when exposed to a moist environment.

At the end of three weeks or so, we had finished most of the cases at Promised Land and English Turn, having rotated back and forth between the two on a regular basis. Bertrandville was still covered in water, but, months later, when it was restored, our assistance would not be needed for it. For Promised Land and English Turn, we had analyzed more than fifty burials. In situations like this, few people are identified through dental records or other traditional means. Much of the identification process is helped along by the family that loved them and carefully placed them in what they hoped was their final resting place. The family members slowly trickled into the center with information about their loved ones, sometimes carrying cards with photos from funeral announcements, sometimes with only the memory of what their loved wore on that last day: a dark blue suit, a striped tie, a bright green dress with a necklace, a purple suit with flowers, a soft cap that hugged the head.

Once the analysis of each burial was complete, the remains were placed within a new casket. Those caskets then had a metal strip bolted to them that identified the person (if possible), and/or listed where the remains were found if identification was not possible. Approximately one-third of the persons who were displaced were identified.

On the last day of the major recovery effort, we packed up all of our supplies, placed them in our vehicles, and said our goodbyes to those faithful few who had stayed to help with the recovery. The last image I had was of Mike Mudge on a large excavator transferring a new casket to the back of the cemetery. We were glad that we could help to recover the dead and try to re-establish where they belonged after Hurricane Isaac destroyed the small communities up and down the river. Great effort would be required to restore these communities to their pre-hurricane state, and, more than likely, some burials would never be found.

We walked away from this effort with a sense that in some small way we had done our part. However, events such as these can stay with you for longer than you first imagined they would. You don't even realize it until the image of a broken casket with someone inside inserts itself into what you thought was an ordinary dream. As time passes, those images appear less often.

15. Cold-Case Database

Though much of our time is spent on active forensic cases that we receive on a regular basis (between forty and forty-five a year), the resolution of some of our cold cases which have been in our laboratory for many years provides us with the incentive to continue our search for the identities of others. This chapter highlights some of those cases.

On September 14, 1992, Mr. John Gagliano, chief coroner's investigator for Orleans Parish, called and told me that someone who was walking through a swampy area near the 11000 block of Chef Menteur Highway in New Orleans had found some bones that looked human. John asked if I could help him with them, and, of course, I agreed.

When the bones arrived in my office, they became case 92-23, the twenty-third case brought to our lab in 1992. I could tell immediately that they had been exposed to the elements for a minimum of a year or so. With only a skull, a scapula, and a few other small pieces, I knew it would be difficult to come up with a full profile to try to get the person identified. I asked John if I could travel to the area where the bones were found to try to find at least one innominate, the hip bone, which is the best bone for determining both sex and age of the person. He said that it had rained so much in the region in the previous weeks that the entire area would be underwater and we would not be able to see anything. He also noted that he thought everything that was associated with the person had been picked up by the coroner's office.

I was concerned that the sex might be hard to assess because the skull was quite small, what we call "gracile," or feminine-like. I knew that it would be somewhat of a challenge to determine for certain if the person was male or female. Back in the early 1990s, DNA profiling that could reveal the X or Y chromosomes was in the future, and no database was available at the time that was accurate enough to determine sex with confidence when based on just the skull. Fordisc software, a powerful tool we use today, was in its infancy at the time and only a promise of the future.

I measured every bone that was measurable, over and over again. Was it a small male, or was it simply a moderately sized female? In the end, my report said "gracile male," which is what my measurements and my visual assessment of the morphology of the skull convinced me was the case. The forehead sloped somewhat (a male characteristic); the root of the zygoma (a raised ridge of bone that in males courses along the temporal bone above the ear hole and often extends just beyond the external auditory meatus) appeared male-like; a few muscle-attachment sites seemed quite prominent for a female (females usually show very little evidence of muscles along certain areas of the cranium, for example, the temporal line—whereas males often do). These features along with the measurements suggested that we were dealing with a male, though there was some concern in the back of my mind.

What about ancestry? That seemed a little more obvious. The sloping eye orbits, the narrow nasal opening, the orthonathic (or straight) appearance of the mid-facial region of the cranium when viewed from a lateral perspective, the towering nasal bones, the prominent anterior nasal spine, all suggested white ancestry.

When I presented the profile to the Orleans Parish Coroner's Office back in 1992 (young, white male), Gagliano informed me they did not have anyone missing who fit the profile of a young white male under the age of thirty. For years, the case languished on the shelf in our laboratory. When we finally began to make progress on the DNA database in 2004, we started with the most recent cases, feeling as though they would be the ones that would have the best chance of getting solved.

As circumstances would have it, in 2010 we were just about to send out the DNA sample for the Menteur swamp case when Susan Burg emailed me and asked if we could determine if our case 92-23 was her brother, John Erickson, who had been missing since August of 1991. At that time, he had called his mother, Alice Woods, from New Orleans and told her he was coming home. The family was very excited because they had not seen him in a while. However, he was never heard from again after the phone call.

Susan wrote to us about how she was drawn to that specific case in our database and how she felt it just had to be her brother. In light of Susan's request to compare the family's DNA to that of our case 92-23, I was especially anxious to have the DNA analysis results on 92-23 because I was still not absolutely certain that it was a male.

I asked Susan to get together with one of our research associates, Helen Bouzon, and work out the details of obtaining DNA from her family to compare to what we hoped would be a full DNA profile from the unidentified person in our lab. Since the skeletal remains had been exposed to the elements for a considerable period of time, for what appeared to be at least a year (all tissue was gone from the remains, and very little odor remained), and the sparse skeletal remains had been in our lab for close to twenty years, I thought the integrity of the DNA might be compromised. Shortly thereafter, however, we were told by the DNA laboratory that our case was indeed that of a male and that they had a full DNA profile. I was elated to see that Y chromosome in the profile.

I was still a little skeptical that our case 92-23 could be Susan's brother, but we never turn down requests from family members to review cases. Both Susan and her mother provided DNA for 92-23. A few months later we were able to tell them that indeed we had a match and that the young man from Menteur swamp was Susan's brother, John Erickson. Of course the family was relieved, but also heartbroken. When a family member is simply "missing," the family holds out hope that the loved one will walk through that door some day and tell them of a great adventure that kept him or her away from home for such a long time. Unfortunately, in most cases, and in the case of 92-23, that was not what happened. On June 23, 2010, we sent John Erickson home to his mother, his sister, and the rest of his family. What happened to John and how and why he was in the swampy area of Chef Menteur Highway remains a mystery which most likely will never be solved.

Another cold case resolved by a hit through CODIS, a rare thing even nationally, began when I received a phone call in September 2008 from the sheriff's office in Lincoln Parish in north Louisiana. A forester was walking in a lightly wooded area just off Highway 80 near Grambling, Louisiana, when he spied some bones. He saw a human skull, and he called the sheriff.

This case was a little different for us in that the sheriff's office thought there was a chance that Lincoln Parish authorities might know who the person was. We made arrangements to meet the sheriff's deputies the next day in Lincoln Parish and prepared for the three-hour trip to the region.

When we arrived in Lincoln Parish, we were escorted by Investigator Byron Feduccia and other officers to a wooded area just off Highway 80, approximately 1.5 miles east of Grambling, Louisiana. The human skeletal remains were only fifteen or twenty yards off the highway. The deputies began to tell the story of the man to whom they might belong. Mr. James David Hunter of Magnolia, Arkansas, fifty-six years of age, was last seen on March 4, 2005. Mr. Hunter periodically visited his brother and others by hitchhiking, often traveling along Highway 80. He would return home the same way. He had not been seen in several years.

The remains scattered before us that day in September 2008 in the lightly wooded area included both hip bones, long bones, the skull, and multiple post-cranial bones. We knew immediately that it was a male from the shape of the hip bone—narrow sciatic notch, sub-pubic convexity, broad ischio-pubic ramus, no ventral arc (a female characteristic). We also knew that he was most likely white by the shape of the skull and that he was older, though we wanted to wait until we had assessed the bones more thoroughly before providing the sheriff with our final profile.

When we got back to the lab and began to process the bones that we had recovered, including several middle rib bones, a troubling discovery was made. According to his brother, Tillman Hunter,

James David Hunter had undergone open heart surgery a few years before he disappeared. But our x-rays and physical examination revealed nothing that would suggest the remains were of a person who had had such a procedure. Generally, open heart surgery requires cutting through the sternum and multiple ribs. Oftentimes, small staples will be used to suture the osseous tissue back together again. Those staples will stay with the person for the rest of his or her life.

I immediately called the sheriff's office and asked for some kind, any kind, of medical records that indicated that Mr. Hunter actually had undergone the operation. All that was available was the testimony from the brother. Since dental records suggested that our case was not a match for James Hunter, we knew that DNA identification was the only way to determine if the remains from the woods were actually his. Tillman Hunter and his sister, Marjorie Hunter, willingly submitted DNA swabs to assist in the identification.

We waited; then we waited some more. News finally came in a couple of months (which is actually fairly quickly since some laboratories require almost a year for DNA confirmation). The DNA was not a match. The remains from the woods were not those of James David Hunter. Then a few weeks later, we received more news, surprising news. A positive identification of the remains from the woods had been made. They were the bones of Mr. Efren Garcia Jr. Garcia had lived in California at some point years earlier and had had some problems that resulted in his DNA being taken and profiled. He had come back to the hills of Louisiana in the recent past, the area where he had lived at one time, the area where he died. His father had reported him missing but died before Garcia was found. A true cold-case hit had been made, one of only three or four for us thus far in our database work. Needless to say, it was an unexpected ending to the case. Mr. James David Hunter of Magnolia, Arkansas, still remains missing.

A final case to demonstrate the power of the DNA database is catalogued as 98-09. On April 16, 1998, I received a phone all from

Dr. Chip Metz, coroner of St. Mary Parish in south Louisiana. Dr. Metz wanted to know if we could provide some help identifying a man whose body had been found in the Atchafalaya River by the operator of a tugboat three days earlier. No one in their area had been reported missing, and authorities had no idea who the man might be. At that time, I was just about to go to one of my classes and asked research assistant Ginny Listi if she could meet Dr. Metz in Morgan City and recover what remains from the body we would need to try to get a positive identification.

Ginny traveled to Morgan City and returned with the remains. After careful evaluation, we were able to say that the man was a mature male, with excellent dental care. He had multiple restorations in his teeth consisting of crowns and fillings, and clearly had visited the dentist on a regular basis. But once again, the old nemesis of ancestry raised its ugly head. In this case, ancestry was somewhat elusive. Some characteristics suggested Hispanic ancestry; others pointed to black ancestry.

Hoping to gain help from Dr. Richard Jantz, of the University of Tennessee, I decided to consult with my old friend and see what he could tell us. Jantz is known internationally, along with Drs. Peer More-Jansen and Steven Ousley, for establishing the Fordisc computer program for determination of ancestry and sex. Over the years, Jantz and Ousley continued to add cases to the database to enhance the accuracy of the program. They had traveled to various laboratories and gathered information on cases from practicing forensic anthropologists all across the country. Additionally, they had asked trusted forensic anthropologists to send them their carefully recorded measurements for cases they had received over the years, thus including even more numbers in the program. Though Fordisc was not yet as powerful in 1998 as it is in 2013, I knew we still needed Jantz's wizardry.

Jantz plugged the numbers for our case 98-09 into what he called his "super program" and came up with a designation of Guatemalan origin. Ultimately, we provided Dr. Metz with a determination that the man pulled from the river a few weeks earlier was an adult male (something he already knew), but of an ancestry that was not quite so simple. We chose "racial admixture," perhaps black or Hispanic in origin.

Fast forward to June of 2005, when the DNA profile for case 98-09, the unidentified male found in the Atchafalaya River, was entered into CODIS. Fast forward again three years later when I received a phone call from Mrs. Tasha Poe, DNA database administrator for the St. Tammany Parish Coroner's Office. Tasha had been notified of a cold-case hit on our case 98-09. The story was almost too hard to believe.

On December 8, 1997, Erica Richardson, a beautiful young pharmacist, was murdered in her home in Florida. Her former boyfriend was John Feiga, who had multiple domestic-violence complaints against him. Richardson's car was missing, and Feiga's truck was found abandoned in Richardson's driveway. Two weeks later, Richardson's car was found abandoned in a hospital parking lot in Lafayette, Louisiana, just sixty miles from John Feiga's home.

Four months later, on April 13, 1998, our case 98-09 was spotted in the Atchafalaya River in St. Mary Parish by a tugboat operator. The abandoned car found in Lafayette was in no way linked to the body of the male found in the river. In June 2008, the FBI entered the foreign DNA found at the crime scene in Florida into CODIS. It hit on our case 98-09. The man from the river was John Feiga. His identification was corroborated by Dr. Robert Barsley, forensic odontologist, with dental records provided by the military, where Feiga had spent a couple of years. Mr. Frank Mula, retired detective for St. Mary Parish, had pursued this case with zeal ever since the body had been found in the river. Once he retired, Detective Scott Tabor took up the gauntlet. Just as diligently, Florida investigators, including Detective Chris Fox, had looked for John Feiga. Feiga's whereabouts were even solicited through the television program *America's Most Wanted.* A cold-case hit from the CODIS database proved invaluable in the partial resolution of this case. John Feiga's death is still under investigation and is not from natural causes.

As more and more family members come forward and provide

Figure 39. Billboard promoting unidentified cold case from 1985.

Figure 40. Billboard promoting unidentified cold case from 2007.

DNA for the national CODIS database, we believe many of the unidentified cases in our laboratory and in other laboratories across the county stand a chance to be sent home. These cold-case hits provide clear evidence of the power of the database and of hope for locating all cases of unidentified and missing persons in each and every state.

In an effort to provide as much publicity for our unidentified cases as possible, a few years ago we entered into a cooperative agreement with Mr. Sid Neuman, director of the regional Crimestoppers group in Baton Rouge. We are working with Lamar Advertising to post images of some of our unidentified cases on billboards across Louisiana. Though none of the five we have posted thus far has resulted in a positive identification, we still believe such advertising can be crucial in getting some of these people identified.

Figure 39 represents a young white female found in 1985 in West Baton Rouge Parish on the banks of the Mississippi River. She was

Figure 41. Crimestoppers playing cards highlighting two of FACES Lab's unidentified persons.

somewhere between twenty-two and thirty-two years of age at death. She wore silver and turquoise jewelry. Figure 40 is a young black female who was found in the Shreveport area in early 2007. She was probably between eighteen and twenty-six. Crimestoppers offers a reward for any information on these cases leading to an arrest and conviction of the perpetrator.

Another project on which we are working with Crimestoppers is to advertise some of our cold cases on the backs of playing cards that the organization has provided to Louisiana prisons. Those are the only cards now allowed in Louisiana prisons. The first printing of several thousand decks of the cards included two of our cases (figure 41). The image on the left is that of a young black male who was found in Natchitoches Parish in 2005. On the right is a young white male who was found in McElroy Swamp in Ascension Parish in 1991. He was probably between the ages of twenty-five and thirty-two. An identifying factor in his case is a small stud earring we found in his ear that was a human tooth encased in a gold setting.

Since there are only fifty-two cards in a deck, Crimestoppers had to select a finite number of cases from each agency with which it is working. The varied cases come from parishes all across the state and include cases of homicide and missing persons. The next printing will include at least two more of our cases. The idea behind the cards is simple. Prisoners will note the cases on the cards as they hold them. Prison gossip may reveal important details about a particular case. This is part of our ongoing effort to keep images of the unidentified persons in our lab in view. The database, the billboards, and the playing cards keep their cases before the public's eye. People love to solve mysteries, and these visual reminders of individuals who are unidentified or are missing give the public an opportunity to become part of the recovery and identification process. The American public is one of our greatest assets.

Epilogue Cases I Always Wanted to Solve

Whether it has been working on modern cases, historic cases, or others, my professional lifetime in forensic anthropology has been the most rewarding career a person could have. I will always be grateful to have been a part of this amazing ride and to have had the opportunity to do something good in this world. As I wind down a long career in forensic anthropology, I think about a few questions that often have been asked of me: "What has driven you all these years, Mary? What is it that makes you pursue your cases with such tenacity? Doesn't seeing all of these dead people bother you?"

Some say that I am like a dog with a bone. I consider that a compliment. Yes, these cases bother me but not in the way some people might think. Typically, I do not dream about my cases, but I do spend a lot of my waking hours trying to resolve some of the more elusive ones. Call it corny or whatever you want to call it, I just want justice for those who can no longer speak for themselves. Justice can mean finding someone who disappeared without a trace; justice can mean identifying those who are held in my lab without a name; justice can mean assisting in some small way to capture a killer. In my more than thirty years of working forensic anthropology cases in Louisiana and across the country, I have had many successes. However, there are many cases that remain unsolved, and I would like to reflect now on a handful of them, some forensic in nature, some bordering on historic.

Obviously, the older a case is, the less likely it is to be solved, but one never knows what answers lie just beyond the next clue. I divide these representative cases into missing-person cases and cases where the victim has been identified but the perpetrator is unknown. Naively, I had hoped that in all of these years I could have helped to solve some of these cases. Unfortunately, that has not happened. Maybe someone will read this epilogue and provide the clue that leads to the resolution of one or more of them. For the peace of mind of their families, I hope that happens. I begin with examples of those who are missing.

In November 1981, Eleanor Parker disappeared without a trace from Baton Rouge. The daughter of a local attorney, Eleanor was a student at LSU and was nineteen years old at the time. She had a part-time job at a popular department store in downtown Baton Rouge, Goudchaux's. Her car was found later on a street in north Baton Rouge. She has never been found.

I had just entered graduate school the year Eleanor disappeared and had begun working with Dr. Doug Owsley on forensic cases that fall. Many years later, I was asked to search a wooded area near the city for Eleanor's body, but I found nothing. Modern DNA technology surely would have proven useful in this case. Her car obviously had been driven and was abandoned in an area that was not near her home. Was there trace evidence in the car that could be reexamined today? Were samples taken that might have foreign DNA on them? Recently, we have been able to obtain DNA from Eleanor's father and sister and have entered that into the CODIS system. Almost thirty years have passed since she disappeared, but we still consider Eleanor when skeletal remains of young white females are found.

In the Louisiana Repository for unidentified and Missing Persons Information Program database is also the case of Rebecca Pauline Gary, who was last seen in Baton Rouge on December 27, 1988. Rebecca was a white female, age thirty-two, approximately five feet two inches tall and weighed somewhere between 105 and 125 pounds. Missing-persons records indicate that she had a tattoo of a lion's head on her right arm. According to a public profile on the web, she was last seen at her apartment on Airline Highway. Some reports have suggested that Gary was having an affair with a former governor of Louisiana; this could not be corroborated. She has not been heard from since that December night.

Gary left behind a young daughter. The daughter's story is that her mother put her on a bus to Shreveport, Louisiana, that night, telling her that there was an envelope under her bed that contained important information should the mother ever go missing. Gary's apartment was searched thoroughly when she could not be contacted. According to accounts, a packed bag and personal items one might need for a trip were still in the apartment. The lights were on in the apartment, but Rebecca Gary had simply disappeared. The envelope was never found.

I have often thought of how Rebecca put her young child on that bus and sent her out of town, perhaps just for a visit with family members, perhaps to protect her. Every time we get a case of a young, unidentified, white female, we consider Rebecca along with the others. Her family has a website dedicated to finding her.

Ylenia Carissi is a third such case. In 1994, she traveled to New Orleans from her home in Italy. The beautiful young woman was from a very wealthy Italian family and was a granddaughter of Tyrone Power, a popular 1940s and 1950s Hollywood movie star. Ylenia was something of an adventurer. Though a rising television star in Italy, she wanted to visit New Orleans and try to become a writer. On January 6, 1994, she disappeared from New Orleans without a trace.

Until 2010, I had never heard of this young woman's case. At that time, a production company from Spain called me and asked if I would do an interview about Ylenia. They were filming a video that would highlight her disappearance from North America's party town. Her tale was most unusual.

As a budding young television actress, Ylenia was Italy's counterpart to Vanna White, star of network television's *Wheel of Fortune* show. At the time of her disappearance, she had been spending some time with Alexander Masakela, a street musician in New Orleans. In fact, according to documents, the two of them had shared a room at the LeDale Hotel in the city. Records indicate that the hotel clerk noted Ylenia had asked for a room with two beds. She had been in New Orleans only for a short time when she simply disappeared.

Authorities investigated her case, following up on a tip that a man had seen a young woman dive into the Mississippi River downtown on the riverfront and that she had run into trouble in the water after a brief period. Did Ylenia, an athlete who was known as a strong swimmer, try, as others before her, to conquer the mighty Mississippi? Was it even Ylenia who jumped into the river that night? For that matter, did anyone jump into the river that night? No body ever surfaced.

What about Alexander Masakela, the musician? He was questioned about Ylenia, was released, and eventually disappeared. At one point, he had even tried to pay a bill with some of her traveler's checks.

Ylenia's family has provided DNA for our missing-persons database. We hope to find her someday.

Finally, two local cases of missing persons stand out in my mind: those of Randi Mebruer of Zachary, Louisiana, and Mary Ann Fowler of Baton Rouge.

Randi Mebruer, a young mother and nurse, disappeared on February 18, 1998. Randi's neighbor saw Mebruer's little three-year-old son riding around on his tricycle outside fairly early one morning with no supervision. She knew something was wrong. Randy adored her son and would not have allowed him to do that. When the neighbor opened the door to Randy's house and saw blood everywhere, she called the police. Her body has never been found. We helped to drain a large pond looking for her but did not find her. DNA from convicted serial killer Derrick Todd Lee was found at her home.

Mary Ann Fowler was kidnapped from a sandwich-shop parking lot on December 24, 2002, as she was heading out of Baton Rouge on a short trip. Video from the store depicts some activity at the scene of her abduction but is lacking clarity. Some have suggested that Derrick Todd Lee may have abducted her. He was thought to be in the general area at the time. Did Lee kidnap her? Mary Ann was more than a generation removed from Lee's other victims, but she looked years younger than her actual age. She has never been found.

Lee and at least one other serial killer were committing such crimes in the region. Perhaps someday Lee will have the compassion to tell Mebruer's family what he did with her body, and if he committed a crime against Fowler, to also confess to that.

Melissa Montz's case is somewhat different from others in that her body was found eventually and she was identified, but the perpetrator is still unknown. Melissa's case is also different in that she was someone I saw on campus on a regular basis. She was a graduate student in the LSU Geology Department in 1985 when I was also a graduate student in anthropology in the same building. I would see Melissa in the hallway now and then and say hello, but I really did not know her well. As a PhD student, she taught introductory courses in geology. Her mentor was Dr. Dag Numendal, LSU professor of geology.

Melissa was known to be an avid jogger. Back in the mid-1980s, though not quite the rage that it is today, jogging around LSU's perimeter was the practice of a considerable number of dedicated enthusiasts. Melissa was among them. Early on a fall morning in 1985, Melissa went jogging and was never seen again. Search parties formed immediately, and the police asked that volunteers mark any region that might reveal anything unusual, like an odd odor, clothing, shoes, and so forth. For days and weeks the volunteers met and marched in all directions, looking for Melissa. Finally, the search ended without finding her. On November 24 of that year, I was spending the afternoon at Broadmoor High School's annual craft fair when, unexpectedly, I heard my name paged. I went to the phone, and it was Dr. Douglas Owsley, forensic anthropologist. He said that someone had found remains that might be Melissa's and asked if I could meet him at the lab. Of course, I agreed.

A man was golfing on the portion of the LSU course near Nicholson Drive when he spotted a dog carrying something in its mouth. Upon closer inspection, the golfer thought it might be a human bone. He called the police, who roped off the area and found the rest of the remains. They were lying in a ditch by the side of the road, just off the trail where Melissa often jogged. Dental records confirmed that the remains were those of Melissa; her death clearly was a homicide. Her murderer has never been found. Was it someone who knew her, or was it simply a crime of opportunity? Melissa's case was the first I worked on of someone I knew, and though it would not be the last, over the years I really hoped that someone might come forward with information about this crime. Thus far, no one has.

What could technology do today that it could not do twenty-five years ago? Not a lot, considering that it had been weeks since her death before Melissa was found. Any DNA evidence left behind at the scene would have deteriorated. A seasoned jogger, Melissa was not slight in appearance. She was at least five feet six or seven inches tall and was a muscular young woman. One cannot help but think that she must have fought hard for her life. Surely, there may have been evidence from the perpetrator under her fingernails. If only she had been found sooner. I look forward to the day when whoever took the life of this promising young woman will be found and convicted.

The case of Dr. Margaret Rose McMillan goes back in time to the 1960s. Her murderer has yet to be found. In 1960, McMillan, a University of New Orleans assistant professor of biology, was found dead on River Road, about six miles south of the LSU campus in Baton Rouge and in close proximity to the Cottage, an antebellum home in the area. Records show that McMillan died of blunt-force trauma to the head, perhaps caused by something such as a tire tool. She was the protégée of Dr. Gregory Mackey, an internationally renowned biologist and head of the LSU Graduate School in Baton Rouge. Allegedly, McMillan was in love with Mackey. In fact, he had been her mentor and more than likely played a role in getting her hired at UNO, which was part of LSU at the time. Mackey was brought before a grand jury with varying pieces of evidence, but the judge at the time dismissed the charges against him. LSU fired him, and he moved to the northeastern part of the country. He died a few years later.

Coincidentally, and one of the more intriguing aspects of this case, the Cottage burned to the ground around the time of the grand jury's inquest into McMillan's death. That home had stood for more than one hundred years and just happened to burn at that time? Interesting coincidence. Did the professor kill McMillan? His wife and son testified that he was home the night of the murder. Today, McMillan lies in her grave, and someone has gone unpunished for her death.

Modern technology would tackle this case with gusto. First, according to some reports, there was a dent in Mackey's car fender. Other accounts note there was a photo of Mackey in McMillan's car. Was it arson that destroyed the Cottage? Had McMillan and Mackey met there? Was someone else there? Was there a witness to the murder? All of the questions remain unanswered. McMillan died just fifty-three years ago. There are people who were living at that time who are still alive today. Perhaps one or more of them knows how to solve this crime.

My final case for reflection is one of the more intriguing ones from a historical perspective. For those of us who spend the better part of our lives associated with LSU, the university becomes a part of who we are. So, understandably, I would be drawn to a case where an LSU professor was actually murdered on one of our campuses. Such was the case of Dr. Oscar B. Turner.

Around 6:00 a.m. on Sunday, June 7, 1925, Louisiana State University Professor Oscar B. Turner walked from his Baton Rouge home near campus to the Agronomy Building. It was the end of the semester, the last semester at the LSU downtown campus, which was in the process of moving to the new campus where classes would begin that fall. It was Turner's last morning on earth. Sometime after 6:00 a.m. he entered the Agronomy Building and was bludgeoned to death by an old ax that had lain around the building for years. Around 8:00 or so that morning, his teaching assistant found him, still alive, on the floor. The ten or more wounds to his head and throat ended his life a few minutes later.

Turner had been at LSU for approximately two years, was something of a loner, and clearly had a larger net worth than the

$200 or so he was paid each month to teach agronomy. Records indicated that he loaned money to reputable people, among them some students. He was also thought to have been involved heavily with real estate speculation for sites around the new campus. Once his financial estate was investigated, some suggested that it might be worth between $30,000 and $100,000, quite a sum of money for the 1920s. Rumors flew. Many people were interviewed and questioned by the coroner's jury. Turner's teaching assistant (who made only $15 a month) was closely scrutinized by the coroner, Dr. W. S. Cushman. Eventually, the assistant was vindicated. A single bloody fingerprint appeared to be all the evidence anyone could find.

Various people came forward with conflicting stories about when Turner actually went to his office that morning (the landlady where he boarded said he left at home at 7:00 a.m., not 6 a.m.); whom he had been seen with lately (one student thought she saw him the day or so before in a large dusty car with three burly men); and why anyone would want to harm such a nice man (he was considered somewhat of a recluse with few close friends, but those who knew him had nothing bad to say about him). His murder was never solved.

So who killed the professor? I have a million questions about this case, but one that has intrigued me has to do with his estate. Where had he come from? He had been at LSU for only two years. Did his money—probably in the neighborhood of what would be around $1 million or more these days—represent an inheritance? Did he step on the wrong toes once he landed at LSU? Indeed, it is a mystery that is almost one hundred years old but one in which modern technology still might play a role. I leave this case and many others to the next generation of forensic sleuths to solve.

Acknowledgments

I thank LSU Press and, especially, Margaret Lovecraft for believing in my work. I thank the anonymous reader for constructive criticism. I thank Stan Ivester for his meticulous final editing. I thank my loving family for their constant support.